GW00674559

MY

FAVOURITE BOOKS

BY

ROBERT BLATCHFORD

1901   LONDON   THE CLARION OFFICE, 72
FLEET STREET, E.C.   WALTER SCOTT LTD.
PATERNOSTER SQUARE, E.C.

TO

WILLIAM RANSTEAD

PREFACE

WHEN my friend Blatchford writes a book, how shall I, who know and love the man as Ben Jonson said he loved Shakespeare—how shall I, I repeat, do aught but praise that book?

But to his letter, in the which he asks me to write a preface, he adds a postscript running thus: "You may send all your praise of this great book to me privately. See?"

I do not see. Walter Besant wrote a book which he called frankly *The Eulogy of Richard Jefferies*. I would eulogise my friend. But if I did he would simply "blue" it. So I will keep my praise for my verbal commendations of the volume.

Avoid books about books, says some sententious soul. For myself, I generally follow that advice. Here in my book-room I can look round on my favourites—Jefferies, Gilbert White, Isaak Walton, Plato, Dickens, Shakespeare, Ruskin, Burns, Shelley, Matthew Arnold, Tennyson, Theocritus, Victor Hugo, Charles Reade, Whitman, Longfellow, Carlyle, Emerson, Wordsworth, Cervantes, Scott,—I write them down just as my eye wanders over the titles,—such friends, such brave companions o' nights when the wind howls without and the ways of the world are full of ruts and mire. I need no guide; I am free of the guild. Every one of them looks down on me invitingly. Thank God — and the strong souls who have left them for us—for good books.

But then a saddening thought: how many do need guides in their choice, and help too, to discriminate between good and bad! All have not had my leisure and opportunities. To such, here is a book in a million. Because, while Mr. Blatchford has only taken a few pearls from his treasury, he has selected carefully, has polished his gems till they are resplendent in the colours in which he sees them, and has put them against just such a foil and with such a light thrown on them that they needs must appeal to us as to him in their glory and their tenderness and purity.

Every man, as he truly tells us, makes his own selection. Some would cavil at my putting Charles Reade down in my list of favourites. Let such re-read the *Cloister and the Hearth*, and swagger through the world, as I do sometimes when I recall its pages, with the cry on my lips—actually on my lips, sometimes in most unexpected and inappropriate places—"*Courage! mon ami! le diable est mort!*" And after Sir John Lubbock included the *Last Days of Pompeii* in his Hundred Best, surely it may be forgiven to anyone to have some favourites who to other people are caviare.

Read no book because you "ought" to read it. I wasted three years on metaphysics, a "Serbonian bog," and five on political economy. To-night I sit with my favourites round me, and as I cannot find time to read, with my twenty odd scapegraces rushing in upon me at every minute of the day, I am fain to take down a volume and rub it tenderly against my cheek. But that is poor consolation for all my wasted years in the Reading Room of the British Museum.

When you get a book that you enjoy, read it aloud. You read more slowly thus; the modern tendency to rush is checked; the memory is strengthened; and you get your author's full measure of power or beauty. *Read aloud.* I am glad that Blatchford asked me to write this preface. The book will be read by so many of my friends, and this introduction gives me the chance of telling you this. I think I'll repeat it: Read your favourites aloud. Poetry especially is written to be read aloud, or, better, sung. The old skald struck his harp and sung his sagas. Thus you get "songs divine, with a sword in every line," the trenchant blade of which cuts keenly through to the marrow of things, and bites down to the innermost recesses of the skald's mind and your own memory. And those stately sentences of Sir Thomas Browne's *Urn Burial*! No one has felt their grandeur to the full who has not *heard* them.

When Hokusai, the great Japanese painter, was very old, he described himself as one who was at length "learning" to draw. But the man can suggest more of rugged strength, or sinuous grace, or swift motion, in one line than most of our royal academicians in a huge canvas. I know next to nothing of the man, but he *must* have lived out o' doors.

Bed books! Give me a book in the sun and the wind, with the sea-gull or the swallow skimming over my head. Out of doors I can talk on equal terms with Shakespeare and Hokusai. The same great elemental forces appeal to all three of us. I too am a man. But abed!—Well, I feel my littleness, and slink abashed behind the counterpane.

Howbeit, come we to cheery old Morley: "Every man to his taste." And, in sooth, if I cannot spend a few minutes with one of my favourites before sleeping, I am fain to pick one up, as I said before, and rub him against my cheek.

Kipling may not be great in the sense of

a creator, but he is the prince and paragon of photographers. And that is no small praise. Blatchford's estimate errs, in my opinion, in this matter. Rudyard Kipling has fired a rifle the echoes of which will reverberate down many generations of our colonial life. That that rifle has often only flashed in the pan, that he has written some painfully weak and puerile things, his best friends will not deny; but that he has greater powers than our author credits him with is my firm and unshakable belief.

"*My*" belief, you see. The personal equation settles most things. It enters more largely into this matter of taste in books than people are willing to admit. The swaggerer will for ever hate Jack Falstaff; the greedy man Sancho Panza. Now I love them all, all the rascals, as does a parson friend of mine those living in his parish. "I love 'em, Lowerison, the villains most of all, perhaps because there is so much of the villain in me."

And that is one of the beauties of wide

reading; it makes one so catholic, so wide-eyed, so gentle with another man's faults. "The wolf, the snake, the hog," says Whitman, "not wanting in me."

And "but for the grace of God" says the tinker of Elstow, looking at a criminal in cart bound for Tyburn, "there goes John Bunyan." Let us all be duly grateful for this "grace of God," and duly humble.

Did you ever leave a good book to hold the baby for your wife or to do a spell of any drudging household work for her? Do you read Charles Dickens' Christmas Books at Christmastide and then go out and look for a Margaret or a Trotty Veck or a Tiny Tim? Because if you don't, you miss what most good books were written for. Not purposely written for, perhaps; but Nunquam sees the picture of the Greek woman in the Art Gallery at Manchester, and then he goes out and meets a poor old woman scavenger of Merrie England staggering under a sack of refuse—and we get a few scathing sentences that sink deep into our hearts who dig the foundation of the "world rebuilded" of

William Morris, and we set our teeth with a firmer determination, and are glad that one work of art told its right tale to the man who could give it voice for us who listen. Yes, the "Art-for-Art's-sake" people may scoff, but give me a book that rouses me to *do* something, to forget myself and strike with what of might there is in me for justice and gentleness and the cause of the poor and the oppressed.

By the way, our author isn't kind to one of my favourites. Years ago, Marxian of the *Labour Leader* and I saved up careful pence for many months to pilgrim to America, steerage fares, and shake Walt Whitman by the hand. We didn't go, because Marxian, who was always doing some silly thing, went and gave his money away to some man who said he wanted it; but if we had gone I was determined to have one baptism over there, or swim across Walden Pond. Instead of which (in choicest Clarionese) Nunquam stigmatises Thoreau as a "puny, greedy, eager soul." So I'll end by slating your book, Master

Nunquam. This isn't true. Thoreau cannot write the English of Gilbert White, but he is just the reverse of what you call him—a big, catholic, wide-eyed, kindly man. Proof? Proofs as plentiful as raisins in a good Christmas pudding in *Walden* itself. Read it again, Nunquam.

. . . . . .

After all, the worst I can say about the book is that it isn't long enough. Nunquam promised some time ago to give us an article on "The Little Flowers of St. Francis." How I wish it could be included in this volume? Couldn't you do it, uncle, at the eleventh hour, for my sake? Certain of your readers have reproached me for that I introduced the book to your notice. I stand in slippery places with these men; set my feet upon the rock before them. And Ruskin isn't noticed here, and stern old dyspeptic Tom, his "dear master," and Omar—such a lot of nonsense is written about Omar to-day, that I sigh for the old days in the eighties when he was only known to a few of us—and mony a mair that I would fain hear Blatchford on. Perhaps he will give us a supplementary volume. Let us hope so. This book whets our appetite; let it also guide some of us in the choice of our dishes.

And so good be with you and with dear old Blatchford. Amen.

HARRY LOWERISON.

RUSKIN SCHOOL HOME, HUNSTANTON,
April 1900.

16

AUTHOR'S NOTE ON THE PREFACE

To read a book in bed is the next best thing to reading it aloud. In the hush of the night one can almost hear the melody of Sir Thomas Browne's sonorous prose, or the chime and music of the *Faerie Queene*.

I do not call Thoreau a "puny soul" positively, but only comparatively. What I object to is his habit of thrusting his ego between us and the landscape. In the presence of the solemn woods and awful heavens *any* human soul is "puny," and Thoreau shows a greedy eagerness to use the immensities as a background for his own self-portraiture.

Gilbert White gave us the flowers and the birds, and kept himself to himself.

Of course I have omitted many books.

B   17

How could I deal with them all? And some of my favourites are too great for me to meddle with. I have neither time nor strength to grapple with *Hamlet, Sartor Resartus, Paradise Lost*, and other giants. And what can I say new about *Pickwick, Don Quixote*, or *Tristram Shandy*?

Papers like those printed here on Gilbert White, Bunyan, and Sir Thomas Browne, cost the writer heavily in time and pains. I could write two novels with less labour than I have spent upon this imperfect, but I hope not wholly useless, book.

R. BLATCHFORD.

HERNE HILL,
April 1900.

CONTENTS

GOOD BOOKS AND BAD BOOKS

Is it possible to tell a good book from a bad one? This curious question was the title of a lecture delivered by Mr. Augustine Birrell in Edinburgh. It is a question more difficult to deal with than one might at first suppose. Mr. Birrell appears to have answered it in the affirmative, but as a lord was in the chair (Lord Rosebery); the newspapers reported the chairman's speech verbatim, and gave the lecturer but a few lines, so that we are but ill - informed as to Mr. Birrell's views.

It seems, however, from some remarks of Lord Rosebery's, that in dealing with poetry Mr. Birrell advocated Matthew Arnold's method of using certain selected verses from the great masters as a sort of touchstone or standard of merit.

On this point several London critics commented, and at least two of them ridiculed Arnold's test. One said it was a fallacy long since exploded ; the other said no one but Matthew Arnold himself had ever taken the suggestion seriously, adding that the absurdity of the idea had been cleverly demonstrated by Lord Rosebery, who remarked that the method worked both ways, and that "a man brought up on Tupper" would condemn Milton.

Does it not seem strange that critics and scholars should be confounded by such a simple issue ?

Matthew Arnold's suggestion was made in 1880 in his general introduction to an edition of the *English Poets*, an article since published in the Second Series of the *Essays in Criticism*. What Matthew Arnold said I will here repeat—

Indeed there can be no more useful help for discovering what poetry belongs to the class of the truly excellent, and can, therefore, do us most good, than to have always in one's mind lines and expressions of the great masters, and to apply

22

them as a touchstone to other poetry. Of course
we are not to require this other poetry to resemble
them; it may be very dissimilar. *But if we have
any tact* we shall find them, when we have lodged
them well in our minds, an infallible touchstone
for detecting the presence or absence of high poetic
quality, and also the degree of this quality, in all
other poetry which we may place beside them. Short
passages, even single lines, will serve our turn quite
sufficiently.

At this point Matthew Arnold gives some
passages as specimen "touchstones" from
Homer, Dante, Virgil, Shakespeare, and
Milton. Those from Shakespeare are
Hamlet's dying request to Horatio—

If thou didst ever hold me in thy heart,
Absent thee from felicity awhile,
And in this harsh world draw thy breath in pain,
To tell my story. . . .

And Henry the Fourth to sleep—

Wilt thou upon the high and giddy mast.
Seal up the ship-boy's eyes, and rock his brains
In cradle of the rude imperious surge. . . .

And now I say again, is it not strange
that any literary man or scholar should

23

question the soundness and efficacy of that method?

For what is all criticism but comparison? Does not every critic tacitly compare every work he reads with some other work of acknowledged merit? In prose and in verse this holds equally true. The novelist is compared to Scott, to Defoe, to Dickens, and praised or censured as he rises towards or falls below the works of those masters.

Universally, Shakespeare is crowned king of poets. And how is the crown awarded? By a method of comparison almost identical with that advocated by Matthew Arnold. Suppose one rose up and declared Tennyson greater than Shakespeare. How should he be refuted but by comparing the work of the two poets and pointing out that Shakespeare's verses excelled the verses of Tennyson?

Declare that Goethe is the greatest creator of character, and at once you will be asked, "Where is Goethe's Hamlet; where are his Falstaff, his Mercutio, his Lear, his Rosalind, his Shylock?" What is this but the method of comparison: the testing of Goethe's power by the "touchstones" of Shakespeare's creative genius?

Turn next to Lord Rosebery's objection that a man "brought up on Tupper" would reject the claims of Milton, and it will be apparent that his lordship is mistaken; nor will it be difficult to discern the cause of his error.

The cause of Lord Rosebery's mistake is at the root of the whole question. "Is it possible to tell a good book from a bad one?" Is it possible for whom? For a man of critical experience and cultivated gift of literary perception; or for a man devoid of taste, experience, or reading?

By no method known could a dunce, or one wholly lacking in literary gift of perception, tell good poetry from bad; nor, on the other hand, could one who understood and loved poetry fail to arrive at a correct verdict after applying Matthew Arnold's method.

A man "brought up on Tupper" (unhappy wretch, if such there be) could only be loyal to Tupper when confronted with Milton by dint of innate incapacity to feel poetry when he heard it. If he clung to Tupper and rejected Milton it would not be because he was "brought up on Tupper," but because he was, in respect of poetical feeling, abnormally dull.

"We needs must love the highest when we see it; not Tupper, nor another." Granted. But how if 'a be blind and *cannot* see it ?

In the line I have italicised, Matthew Arnold gives a hint of this. He says of the quoted passages : "but if we have any tact . . . we shall find them an infallible guide. . . . "

And later in the essay he repeats the qualification, saying, "These few lines, if we have tact and can use them, are enough even of themselves to keep clear and sound our judgments about poetry."

I say again, there seems no surer way than Arnold's. About the relative merits of different pieces of great poetry, about the relative ranks of great poets, there is ample room for argument, but as to the question of whether a piece of **poetry** be great or only mediocre, it would **appear that there is** no room for doubt whatever—if **we have** any *tact*.

So much for poetry. Next as to prose. Can one tell a good **book from a bad one?** That depends who is the **judge, and what** is the quality of his **judgment.** Some reviewers have classed **Stevenson and even** Crockett above Walter **Scott, and lauded** Stanley Weyman as the **master of Defoe.** The other day a London **reviewer singled** out a character from the **puppets of a new** novel as worthy to go **down to posterity** "by the side of Uncle Toby." These are gross errors, and strong evidence that some, and of those who profess judgment, are incapable of telling a good book from a bad one.

But all men are not equally dull of perception, nor equally inexperienced. Some have natural "tact," to use Arnold's word, in literature, and of those some have culti-vated their gift by study and observation. To such men it is easy to tell a good book from a bad one; nay, it is well-nigh impossible for such men ever to mistake a bad book for a good one.

Let us take fiction, and try to find some foundations upon which to base a judgment.

We have in such work two things to consider: the matter and the manner. In some books the matter is better than the manner, in other books the manner is better than the matter.

As to both matter and manner, the chief essentials of greatness, it seems to me, are originality and strength. No new style is a great style which is an echo of the style of another writer. A great style must not only be a good style, it must be an original style. Stevenson's style is good, it is beautiful, polished, brilliant, but it is not great. Whereas the style of Dickens is faulty, unequal, sometimes even slovenly, but *great.*

As to this matter of style again, let the student ask himself of his author is it clear, is it forcible, is it graceful, is it euphonious? Does the writer wallow in platitudes and

28

cliches? Does he use weak or hackneyed similes? Is his metaphor mixed, or unapt, or stale? Is his wit cheap or obvious? All these are the marks of a bad style; but there are many more, and their opposites are the marks of a good style. Easy enough to determine these questions—provided we have *tact* and knowledge.

When we come to matter we come to a question of much wider scope. But here again we need not be in doubt as to the choice between a good book and a bad one. As apart from quality of style (or manner), where are the chief essentials of greatness in fiction? For what are we to seek in the *matter* of such literature?

The essentials of greatness in fiction are, I should say, originality, strength, and insight. The chiefest test of greatness in a novelist lies in his power to create character.

Scott is great. He is admittedly great. Let us ask, then, as to his creation of character. Has he created any great characters? If so, has he created many great characters? The answer comes pat. As M. Davidson once said to me, Scott has been excelled by no writer save Shakespeare in the creation of character. Not only has he created great characters, but he has created them with marvellous ease, with singular truth, and in prodigal numbers. There they are before us for ever, an unsurpassed gallery of human portraits, all original, all striking, and all true.

There are kings, queens, soldiers, courtiers, robbers, peasants, Puritans, priests, knights, gipsies, ladies, seamen. All vivid, all natural, all new. Name but a few of them, and the master stands revealed. Compare Louis XI. and Charles II., Balfour of Burleigh and Dugald Dalgetty, Claverhouse and the Dougal Creature, Jeanie Deans and Amy Robsart—nay, it would take more space than I have to spare even to print the names of the great creations of the Wizard of the North.

My good friend, John Morrison Davidson, chatting with me about Walter Scott, claimed that Dugald Dalgetty, as a character creation, was equal to Falstaff. Now, Morrison

Davidson is a sound critic, and Dalgetty is a masterpiece of characterisation, but I find myself unable to agree to this bold claim. But before I compare the two characters, I will say a few words on the more general subject of the characterisation of our two great creators of human nature.

I think Shakespeare is Scott's master in beauty and in humour, though Scott's fidelity to nature is unexcelled.

For instance, I prefer Shakespeare's women to Scott's. They are not only wittier and more generally intellectual, but they are more sweet and gracious. Nor is this superior grace due solely to the poetic beauty of their diction. Ophelia, Rosalind, Hermione are sweet at the core, they are innately delicate and lovely. Di Vernon is not such a "lady" as Rosalind, and Jeanie Deans appears homely and undistinguished in the presence of the flower-like daintiness, the tender grace, and the wistful beauty of Ophelia.

Shakespeare had the greater and more ethereal imagination of the two great makers of men and women : that, I take it, is the reason why the characters of Scott are earthier.

Nor shall we say that the nearer the earth, the nearer human nature ; for man is blended of earthly clay and heavenly fire, and the artist who paints the soul is nobler than he who paints the mind and the fleshly form.

Come we now to Dugald Dalgetty and Falstaff.

Both these are men of very imperfect natures. Falstaff is the grosser, the more culpable. Dalgetty has more honour than the fat Knight, more honour and fewer vices. And yet we love Falstaff, while we do not love Dalgetty. It would seem that our old white-bearded Satan, our globe of sinful continents, our reverend vice and grey iniquity, has given us medicines to make us love him. But the reason is that while Dugald's selfishness and heartlessness repel us, the still greater frailties of Falstaff are made to show tenderly through a glamour of wit and jollity. Surely if that be so our

Shakespeare scores one, for is it not the very mark of genius that he has made us better love the less worthy of two men?

But let us proceed in a more systematic manner, and try to discover, if we can, some fixed principles upon which the various characters in fiction may be judged and compared with each other.

To deserve the rank of a great creation, a character should be not only a true type of his class, his trade, and his nationality, but also an original specimen of the human race.

Thus, Silas Marner, besides being an excellent type of a North of England weaver of his day, is also a strongly marked, distinctly novel, and vividly interesting personality.

So a soldier of fortune, like Dalgetty, must be a strongly marked human type, as well as a truly drawn military type of Scot. So Sir John, besides being a true type of courtier, roysterer, and adventurer, must be also a new type of man.

The common error of the smaller author in portraying class or national types is the

C   33

error of exaggeration and the excess of mannerism. We all know the typical Irishman, the typical sailor, and the typical rustic of cheap fiction. It is easy to build or to copy such counterfeits.

Great authors seldom fall into such error. Scott, I believe, never exaggerates, Shakespeare seldom, although in such characters as those of Dogberry and Llewellen one might claim that he had let his riotous and vigorous humour have too much its will of the rein.

Great creations should also be true to their own nature. All that Falstaff does and says is like himself (I beg we may pass lightly over *The Merry Wives*), and Dalgetty is Dalgetty always.

Here Scott is above reproach. His characters are consistently true to themselves in all cases. He never yields to the weakness of falling in love with his own creations, as Dickens did. Dugald Dalgetty has a kind of affection for his well-tried, war-worn battle steed. But when the charger is killed the canny Scot stops on the battlefield to skin

34

him. The hide will make an excellent coat of defence against the cruel climate of the hills. Dickens would have made Dalgetty weep over the horse's body. Scott's genius is too sane and true.

Compare the Mr. Pickwick of the Fleet with the Mr. Pickwick who has the quarrel in the club. There is a complete change of nature. Natures do change. Yes. But the author should show cause. It is quite in keeping that Falstaff should make a good end, and that he should babble of green fields. There was a native softness and religious awe in the man, as in the time; but Mr. Pickwick's development into an angel in gaiters is more questionable. At the outset the gaiters were more pronounced, and the wings less visible.

Well, then, we may lay it down as a rule that a great creation should be a true type of his class, and a new and striking type of his race.

Let us, then, consider a few cases in point.

There is the matchless pair of old soldiers

—captain and corporal — Uncle Toby and his servant Trim.

The first of these is an officer and a gentleman, the second is a soldier and a man. Both are startlingly original and convincing, both gloriously humorous and tenderly compelling. The heart of Toby Shandy is brimful of the milk of human kindness, and his head is a lumber-room of battles and sieges, of bombs, trenches, mines, assaults, and sudden death.

The corporal is so true a soldier that his image may be found in the ranks of any British regiment to-day. His heart is soft also, and his mind a comical magazine of quaint follies, human frailties, and amazing misconceptions.

But I must escape from the toils of Sterne. Where in all literature is there such a cast of characters as the cast of *Tristram Shandy*? Where is such a varied and delightful bouquet of humours? — Mr. and Mrs. Shandy, My Uncle Toby, and the widow Wadman, Corporal Trim and Bridget, Dr. Slop and Yorick, with their amazing controversies, their impossible philosophies, their side - splitting cross purposes, and crooked answers. And despite all eccentricities, absurdities, and freakish fancies, what perfect truth to nature, what tenderness and sweet goodwill.

Sancho Panza and Don Quixote are an immortal pair, Falstaff and his satellites, Bardolph, Nym, and Ancient Pistol, Mrs. Quickly, Poins, and the boy, are a galaxy of humorous glories, and perhaps there is no such masterly comic painting extant as the scene in Shallow's garden where Sir John and Bardolph, the Justice and Silence, and the Ancient of heroic speeches foregathered. For here are some half-dozen great humorous creations, all distinct in character, all original, and no one of them thinking the thought or speaking the language of any other.

Yet even this masterly company lack the subtle sweetness, the spiritual gentleness, the elusive tenderness of the Shandy troupe. No humorist I know could sweeten and soften his laughter with the delicate perfume of loving - kindness as did Laurence Sterne.

Milton made the devil a gentleman : what would he have been in the hands of Tristram Shandy ?

Perhaps next to Sterne no author has handled human faults more gently than Robert Browning. Fra Lippo Lippi is not only a marvellous study of character: it is also a sermon on Christian charity, and an example of love in laughter.

On consideration, then, it seems that, judging Falstaff and Dalgetty by the rules I have presumed to frame, we must give the palm to Shakespeare.

For, whereas Dalgetty is a perfect type of the Scottish soldier of fortune in his day, it must, I think, be admitted that he is more like *other* soldiers of fortune of his day than Sir John Falstaff is like other fat knights of *his* day. I claim, in short, that Shakespeare's man is more humorous, more lovable, more witty, more original, than the creation, masterly though that creation be, of the wonderful Wizard of the North.

This matter of characterisation is of such moment in fiction that we cannot consider it too carefully. For it is easy to fall into misconceptions that will warp or impair our critical judgment. Thus, I find an American professor excusing Kipling for the poverty of his characterisation upon the ground that "being primarily a short-story writer, he is by the definition of his art excluded from triumphs of this kind, since characterisation requires a larger canvas."

But surely it is a mistake to assume that character drawing requires a large canvas. True, the modern American school of stipplers need a whole acre to paint a cow in, but it is not so with the masters. The whole of the scenes in which Falstaff appears in the first part of *Henry IV.* do not contain above 14,000 words. I should say that in 20,000 words Shakespeare has elaborated the characters of all that wonderful galaxy of humours : Falstaff, Bardolph, Nym, Pistol, Dame Quickly, Justice Shallow, Prince Hal, and Poins. And how much canvas do Dogberry and Verges fill, and the Gravediggers in *Hamlet*? Could not Ophelia, and

39

Polonius also, be put into the space of a short story? And what of Rip Van Winkle, and Trotty Veck, and the members of "Sleary's Horsemanship"? And in how many words does Browning paint the wonderful portraits of Fra Lippo Lippi and Andrea del Sarto? If it comes to that, Kipling has, in Mother Pummeloe, the soldier matron, drawn a very fine character upon a very small canvas. No. It is not acreage that is needed, but brains.

It is not by counting the pages that we shall be able to tell a good book from a bad one.

OF BED BOOKS

IF the reading of good books is ever sinful, it is at meal‑times. He who reads at meal-times treats his meal and his digestion with discourtesy, and puts upon his author the affront of a divided allegiance. But to read in bed! That is a good man's virtue, the innocent indulgence of the well-deserving. Therefore gossip about bed books will ever be acceptable to the just. And the wise man will show a nice discrimination in the choice of his literary nightcap. It is a case of means and ends. A man might write about bed books until he sent his readers to sleep, yet would get no "forrader" unless he followed some logical plan.

Do you want to go to sleep or to keep awake? That is the question. Are you a reader, or only one who reads? Do you love books, or would you e'en be snoring?

A gentleman, look you, would fain go to sleep like a gentleman. That is leisurely, kindly, with a grateful smile to Goodman Day, his host that is, and a graceful greeting to Mistress Night, his hostess that is to be. None but a boor would turn his back upon the sun in churlish haste, and jump into the arms of Morpheus neck and crop, like a seal rolling off an ice-floe. Therefore, a gentleman reads before he goes to sleep.

The ideal bed book should be small, printed in good type, not too boisterous, not too sad; an old friend. Then, with a mild, clear light, a pipe, and something in a tumbler, a man may court happiness, and win her; and the malice of the gods and follies of the flesh shall fret his soul no more.

The best bed book I know is Spenser's poems. That is a book you cannot fully appreciate in the workaday hours. Only in the silence of the night can one hear the murmur of its song, like the regular irregularity, the ordered wildness, and chiming cadence of a brook—

> Along the shore of silver-streaming Thames,
> Whose rutty bank, the which his river hems,
> Was painted all with variable flowers,
> And all the meads adorned with dainty gems,
> Fit to deck maidens' bowers,
> And crown their paramours
> Against the bridal day, which is not long:
> Sweet Thames, run softly, till I end my song.

Brook, quotha? Did I say brook? No. Here we have the strong sweep and full-throated gurgle of the brimming, singing river—

> Of every sort which in that meadow grew,
> They gathered some; the violet pallid-blue,
> The little daisy that at even closes,
> The virgin lily, and the primrose true,
> With store of vermeil roses,
> To deck their bridegroom's posies
> Against the bridal day, which was not long:
> Sweet Thames, run softly, till I end my song.

The river, the lipful, flowing, sweet, melodious river. Who knows e'er a finer tide on which to float into Poppyland?

I do not recommend novels as bed books.

43

Not even novels which the reader knows. (New novels are, for obvious reasons, as impossible at the bedside as a comet solo.) But if I did indulge in a nightcap of Thackeray's, or Scott's, or Dickens' brewing, I should select for night all the parts I should skip by day : I mean the descriptions, reflections, and digressions from the beaten way of narrative.

No. We want singers, talkers, tattlers, prattlers at our pillow. A bed book must be a well-bred fellow, a fellow of culture, of good grace ; soft-spoken, cheerful, politely reticent. A man does not go to bed to be bullied, roared at, roused to mutiny, deceived into tears, nor yet to be preached to death by wild curates. Longfellow was thinking of bed books when he wrote "The Day is Done"—

> Then the night shall be filled with music,
> And the cares that infest the day
> Shall fold their tents, like the Arabs,
> And as silently steal away.

And, indeed, among bed books Longfellow's own poetry ranks high.

Bed books, when in prose, should be of the "dipper" class—such as one may cut and come again.   Next to Spenser, I should place Sir Thomas Browne—especially *Urn Burial.* Then, of poets, Omar Kháyyám; *The Earthly Paradise;* Shakespeare's *Sonnets;* Browning's *Lyrics*—especially "Fra Lippo Lippi" and "Andrea del Sarto"; and Shelley's "Alastor."

What nobler nightcap could man desire than the magnificent invocation—

Earth, ocean, air, beloved brotherhood ;
If our great mother has imbued my soul
With aught of natural piety to feel
Your love, and recompense the boon with mine ;
If dewy morn, and odorous noon, and even,
With sunset and its gorgeous ministers ;
And solemn midnight's tingling silentness ;
If autumn's hollow sighs in the sere wood,
And winter robing with pure snow and crowns
Of starry ice the grey grass and bare boughs—
If spring's voluptuous pantings when she breathes
Her first sweet kisses—have been dear to me . . .

What better talk than that do we crave—

When night makes a weird sound of its own
   stillness?

45

It is the perfection of bedside music.

Milton's "Allegro" and "Penseroso" are all one could wish; but beware lest you be drawn into the maelstrom of *Paradise Lost*, which is about as suitable for the bedchamber as the reverberating roll and thunder of the massed drums of the whole brigade of Guards.

"Hiawatha," now, is the glass of nightcap fashion and the mould of bedroom form. Especially the lovely prelude, with its forest echoes, its wild-pine odour, its sweet human tenderness and noble catholic toleration—

> Ye who love a nation's legends,
> Love the ballads of a people,
> That like voices from afar off
> Call to us to praise and listen,
> Speak in tones so plain and childlike,
> Scarcely can the ear distinguish
> Whether they are sung or spoken,
> Listen to this Indian legend,
> To this song of Hiawatha !
> Ye whose hearts are fresh and simple,
> Who have faith in God and Nature,
> Who believe, that in all ages
> Every human heart is human,

> That in even savage bosoms
> There are longings, yearnings, strivings
> For the good they comprehend not,
> That the feeble hands, and helpless,
> Groping blindly in the darkness,
> Touch God's right hand in that darkness,
> And are lifted up and strengthened ;—
> Listen to this simple story,
> To this song of Hiawatha !

Could one fall asleep to a more melodious lullaby, or close the day with gentler thoughts ?

As to prose, we must have Montaigne's *Essays*, and enjoy the old knight's quaint wisdom and startling candour ; nor can we spare the whimsical humour, smiling frankness, and genial irony of *The Sentimental Journey*; and I should certainly advise the selection of the *Journal to Stella*, which, as love-letters and old-time gossip, is unique.

I admit that the perusal of love-letters sent to a woman dead a century and a half ago smacks eerily, but were there ever such letters written ?—

> I have been scribbling this morning, and I believe I shall hardly fill this side to-day, but send it as it is ;

and it is good enough for naughty girls that won't write to a body, and to a good boy like Presto. I thought to have sent this to-night, but was kept by company, and could not; and to say the truth, I had a little mind to expect one post more for a letter from M. D. . . . Parvisol tells me he can sell your horse. Pray let him know that he shall sell his soul as soon. What? Sell anything that Stella loves, and may sometimes ride? It is hers, and let her do as she pleases, . . . let him sell my grey, and be hanged . . .

It is wonderful, the soft playfulness, the strange tenderness of that saturnine and bitter man. Swift's love-letters put me often in mind of a panther fondling its cubs.

Well, let me see, we want the Bible to read Job, Ecclesiastes, and the Song of Solomon; we want Burton's *Anatomy of Melancholy*, Ritson's *Robin Hood, Quaint Old Ike*, a volume of De Quincey, and the *Banquet of Plato*; and I think we shall get good entertainment out of Thackeray's *Roundabout Papers*, Landor's *Imaginary Conversations*, and Andersen's *Fairy Tales*. I don't read the real fairy tales; but the wistful, dainty blend of humour and pathos

48

in such sketches as "The Bottle Neck" and the "Bachelor's Nightcap" make a feast for a king.

And then, to break our own rule, I must plead for *Hamlet* and *Sartor Resartus.* I think we must admit *Hamlet* for the peerless poetic beauty of the speeches, and *Sartor* because of its mystery and its music, the sardonic humour playing over sorrowful deeps, like lightning on dark seas, and for the sake of the sweet strength and keen insight of the weird old doctor's verbal nocturne over the sleeping city.

These are nearly all old books. Good bed books are mostly old. The moderns are in too great haste. A bed book should be written at leisure. Hurry is fatal; leisure and repose essential. Look at the *Urn Burial!* Look at Burton's *Anatomy of Melancholy!* The makers of bed books wrote for love, not for money. The incentive of gain does not result in the production of bed books. It results in the halfpenny newspaper, the scrappy magazine, the factory system, the slums, and the apotheosis of the opulent lower orders. *The Imitation of Christ* would not suit *Tit-Bits*, nor could *The Earthly Paradise* have been produced at so much a line. Pot-boilers and smart paragraphs will not harmonise with "solemn midnight's tingling silentness." The *Daily Telegraph* belongs to the train; in bed we prefer the Song of Solomon, or the *Table Talk of Selden.*

An excellent book to read in bed is Blackmore's *Tales from the Telling House.* Blackmore in his quieter moments has the leisured ease, the high-bred serenity of the older writers. In these moments his style is ripe, graceful, charming. In this book the tales are not very strong tales, nor are they very strongly told; but the pure English, the graceful style, and the author's gentle and sunny good-humour are irresistible. Who can deny a chuckle of enjoyment to the account of the Welsh quarrymen who were "a thoroughly civil, obliging, and rather intelligent set of men; most of them also of a respectable and religious turn of mind; and they scarcely ever poach, except on

Saturdays and Mondays"? Who can fail to
relish the description of the gentleman well
up in the Treasury, who was knighted for
"finding a manuscript of great value that
went in the end to the paper mills"? Says
Mr. Blackmore, with his quiet smile, "How
he did it, or what it was, or whether he ever
did it at all, were questions for no one to
meddle with. People in those days had
larger minds than they ever seem to exhibit
now. The king might tap a man, and say,
'Rise, Sir Joseph,' and all the journals of
the age, or, at least, the next day, would echo
'Sir Joseph.' And really he was worthy of
it. A knight he lived, and a knight he died,
and his widow found it such a comfort."

So did the widow's son, for the merry
author tells us : "He, by some postern of
influence, got into some dry ditch of the
Treasury, and there, as in an old castle
moat, began to be at home, and move, gently
and after his seniors, as the young ducks
follow the old ones. And at every waddle
he got more money." Which is very refresh-
ing to the jaded reader.

But the most delightful tale in the book is "Crocker's Hole," which is simply the story of a schoolboy who catches a trout. I do not favour fishing, which I cannot help feeling is cruel; but the "telling" of this tale is a treat no book-lover can afford to miss. Here the style is of the author's best, the raillery light as the tickling of a fly's wing, the descriptions masterly, and the realisation of local atmosphere a feat of magic. Blackmore nearly always takes us out into the open air, and few writers have shown more skill in painting still life, or such a gift for caging sunshine, wild wind, leaping water, and waving grass within the black bars of a book. In proof of which take this fine artistic picture of the great trout in "Crocker's Hole":—

His head was truly small, his shoulders vast; the spring of his back was like a rainbow when the sun is southing; the generous sweep of his deep, elastic belly, nobly pulped out with rich nurture, showed what the power of the brain must be, and seemed to undulate, time for time, with the vibrant vigilance of his large wise eyes. His latter end was consistent also. An elegant taper run of counter, coming

52

almost to a cylinder, as a mackerel does, boldly developed with a hugeous spread to a glorious amplitude of swallow tail. His colour was all that can well be desired, but ill described by any poor word-palette. Enough that he seemed to tone away from olive and umber, with carmine stars, to glowing gold and soft pure silver, mantled with a subtle flush of rose and fawn and opal.

There, could Gilbert White have done it better. And the whole tale is equally good. Read the account of the dancing of the may-fly on the water, and of the emerald beetle asleep in the heart of the rose :—

And when the sunlight breaks upon his luscious dissipation, few would have the heart to oust him, such a gem from such a setting. All his back is emerald sparkles; all his front red Indian gold, and here and there he grows white spots to save the eye from aching.

And that reminds me. Once in Fleet Street I saw a shabby and dejected man bow to a couple of radiant and stylish advertisement canvassers. When the man had passed one canvasser said, " Who's that feller?" "Oh!" said the other, "he's a literary chap. One of those descriptives, you know. A feller that writes half a column about a hen crossing the street."

Those superior men of ads. would not, perhaps, approve of the dainty skill of "Crocker's Hole," but we know better.

There is a good half - crown edition of Blackmore by Sampson, Low, Marston, & Co. Get *Lorna Doone* and *Tales from the Telling House*, and say it is my fault if you don't like them.

As for a list of bed books—I could a tale unfold; but let every man court the mistress that best likes him.

A SERAPHIC BOOK

WE value some books for their shrewd wisdom, others for their spiritual sweetness. Some please us by their dainty wit, their gaiety or quaintness; others charm us with delicate fancies, or by strange qualities of wistful tenderness touch us softly.

The styles and characters of books are as various as the souls and humours of the women and men who made them. We play with one as the children played with Rip Van Winkle; we gossip with another as Rosalind gossiped with Celia, or Pendennis with Warrington. To some we doff our hats, to some we kiss our hands, and those in all the differently whimsical, civil, or gallant ways in which hands may be kissed or hats lifted. There are those with whom we would fain argue keenly, and those in whose jovial

55

company we give ourselves up to wholesale and heart - cleansing laughter. To others, again, we listen with bitter-sweet feelings of blended hope and sadness, as Cœur de Lion listened behind his bars to the songs of Blondel.

Now an author whom we may love lightly, jest with easily, hobnob with gaily, flirt with handsomely, laugh with freely, bow to with gentle and quiet gravity, or sigh over wistfully without too sharp a pain, is the kind of friend one may ask to sit by one's pillow when one's mind is ruffled or disquieted and the soft-bosomed goddess of sleep is coy.

Such friends at need are Gilbert White and Thomas Mallory, Emerson, Lamb and Matthew Arnold, Boswell, and Plato and Robert Louis Stevenson—men whose voices are refined and gentle, whose smiles cheer, whose words delight and heal. Happily there are many such; so many that one might draw out the list like Duncan's line. Indeed, the indulgent reader will miss many of his dearest from the above brief roll; as I do. But this is not a catalogue, nor when

one pays tribute to the radiance of the
dewy Venus or the Ruby Mars, does one
despitefully use, or faithlessly ignore the
golden splendour of Jupiter, or the scin-
tillating loveliness of that celestial diamond,
Sirius the multi-coloured. No son of Adam
could in one mouthful hold all the sins his
conscience groans for, and what daughter of
Eve may crowd into one bride's confession
the full tale of the flirtations her heart
knoweth? Neither can I write here the
names and titles of all the books and authors
who have helped me to defy those memorial
"ghosts and sprites that haunt the nights,"
when the mind is wakeful or the soul sad.

Of Rabelais as a bedside friend I have
spoken before. I propose now to introduce
two others, both vastly different from the
Pantagruelian satirist and Gargantuan
laugher, and each as different from the
other. Just now I said that we value some
books for their shrewd wisdom and some
for their spiritual sweetness. Here is a book
of each kind—to wit, the *Table Talk of John
Selden* and the *Letters of Samuel Rutherford.*

Selden, the English lawyer, was practical, moderate, and acute. Rutherford, the Scots divine, was spiritual, enthusiastic, and eloquent. The former was born in 1584 and died in 1654; the latter was born in 1600 and died in 1661.

Both were contemporaries of Milton, Sir Thomas Browne, and Raleigh; both strove and laboured, met with rewards and persecutions in the fierce and strident times between the First James and the Second Charles; both wrote in a period when English prose was in the making, the influence of the Elizabethan masters' genius being still powerful, although the germs were already visible from which were to be evolved the styles of Hobbes and Dryden.

Let us deal first with that brave and tender reincarnation of Thomas à Kempis, Samuel Rutherford.

Samuel Rutherford was born at Nisbet, in Roxburghshire, in the year 1600, about the time when the Globe Theatre flourished, and when Bacon was engaged upon his *Advancement of Learning* and Cervantes

upon *Don Quixote*. Selden was then sixteen years of age, and was studying in the
Temple. Elizabeth was still on the throne,
and Raleigh in the Tower. The *Faerie
Queene*, Bacon's *Essays*, and *The Merchant of
Venice* were new books in vogue, and rare
Ben Jonson with his boon companions held
wassail at the Mermaid. Cromwell was
then a baby in arms (who can so picture
the grim, steel-hearted Lord Protector?),
Charles the First was a baby unborn, and
many evils and terrors yet undreamed of
were looming up towards the horizon. The
liberty of speech and conscience so cheap
and so lightly held to-day were then un-
fought for, and the round-eyed infant lying
in the Roxburghshire cradle with the seeds
of faith and valour yet dormant in his heart
was verily born to trouble as the sparks fly
upward.

Educated at Jedburgh and Auld Reekie,
Samuel Rutherford took his M.A. degree
at Edinburgh in his first year of manhood,
and became minister of Anwoth Parish
Church at twenty-seven.

In 1636 the minister of Anwoth got into disfavour, Charles the First having blossomed into a king, and was for conscience' sake banished to Aberdeen.

At Aberdeen, during his two years' exile, Rutherford wrote most of the letters in this volume. In 1638 he was restored to Anwoth Church, and in 1639 was appointed Professor at St. Andrews and Principal of New College.

For some years he flourished in peace, working diligently and studying with zeal, so that it was said of him: "He is *always* praying, *always* preaching, *always* visiting the sick, *always* catechising, *always* writing and studying," and, may be now added, *always* setting a golden example of life well lived and work done faithfully. Thus it was he grew in grace, thus it was he exercised a great and wholesome influence on the Church of Scotland. He was a Commissioner of that church from 1643 to 1647, wrote many works, chiefly theological, and is supposed to have been the author of the original of the historic "Shorter Catechism."

After the Restoration, Rutherford again incurred displeasure in high places. In 1661, the year in which Cromwell's body was exhumed and gibbeted at Tyburn, Rutherford had the honour (for it was an honour in that licentious reign) of having one of his books burnt by the common hangman. In the same year he was deprived of his offices, and summoned to appear before the Scottish Parliament.

But Rutherford was dying, and to the summons sent back the courageous reply that he was already summoned to a higher tribunal, adding with cool Scottish humour, "I behove to answer my first summons; and ere your day arrive I will be where few kings and great folks come."

This answer was not to the taste of Parliament, who solemnly and egregiously voted that he should not be allowed to die in the college. Whereupon up rose Lord Burleigh, saying, "Ye cannot vote him out of heaven."

So, with the harness on his back, died that brave Christian soldier.

There is, so far as I am aware, no portrait of Samuel Rutherford extant, and we must make mind-pictures of him as we may from the following slight indication contained in a letter of an English merchant who once saw him and heard him at St. Andrews.

"I came," the merchant says, "to Irvine, and heard a well-favoured, proper old man (David Dixon) with a long beard, and that man showed me all my heart. Then I went to St. Andrews, where I heard a sweet, majestic-looking man (R. Blair), and he showed me the majesty of God. After him I heard a little fair man (Samuel Rutherford), and he showed me the loveliness of Christ."

Rutherford has been well called "a little master of English"; his *Letters* have won from many the proud title of "the most seraphic book in our literature." In these two phrases we have the essential characteristics of Rutherford as a writer and a man.

To us, as friends and students, the chief qualities of this book are its style and its spiritual enthusiasm. Both qualities are vividly revealed in the following short passage from one of the letters :—

A little of God would make my soul bankfull. Oh that I had but Christ's odd off-fallings; that He would let but the meanest of His love-rays and love-beams fall from Him, so as I might gather and carry them with me. I would not be ill to please with Christ, and vailed vision of Christ; neither would I be dainty in seeing and enjoying of Him : a kiss of Christ blown over His shoulder, the parings and crumbs of glory that fall under His table in heaven, a shower like a thin May-mist of His love, would make me green, and sappy, and joyful, till the summer-sun of an eternal glory break up.

There you have Samuel Rutherford. The "little master of English," using his mastery to put his fervid faith and burning spiritual zeal into prose as sweet as song.

Rutherford, as I have said, was a religious enthusiast. He is akin to Thomas à Kempis and St. Francis d'Assisi. To us, reared in these self-contained and undemonstrative times, there is something startling in his daring metaphors and passionate adoration—

One smile of Christ's face is now to me as a kingdom. . . . He holdeth up my head, and

63

stayeth me with flagons of wine, and comforteth me with apples. My house and bed are strewed with kisses of love.

Such fiery faith, such spiritual exaltation are rare in the world and precious. Without faith man is a mere husk. For his health's sake, for his life's sake, it is fit he should believe in something,—in a mother, a wife, a sweetheart, a friend, a hero, a cause,—it is the act of faith, the human trust that is admirable and beneficial.

And what would the world be without its enthusiasts, or life without enthusiasms? This fitful fever, this yoke-bearing drudgery under goad, which all of us endure, is not our real life. We submit to it, without accepting it. We do not love it, nor believe in it. Our real world is one of dreams: we dwell in airy castles, and our joys are in our aspirations. It is as though Plato was right, and we get our souls from a more perfect state, and with them some pale memory of what is true and noble—a faint yearning for something purer and sweeter than the earthly fact. The vilest sinner despises sin; the most arrant knave perceives that honour is better than villainy. Men work in grime and dirt, but every man loves to have his body clean. Fallen, degraded, blunted, and given over to the seivice of Baal we may be ; but if amid the dust and clatter of the devil's workshop one true note is sounded, our debauched memory stirs itself, our dull wits wake and listen.

Is it not sad to mark so many human failures — so many lamps burnt dim and fountains muddled ? Is it not tragic when the faded eyes of age look back upon the ashes of burnt-out enthusiasms—the skeletons of faiths that died ? With what hope of soul and gaiety of heart we set out on the voyage to the sunny shores which few eyes but the young can see. But woe betide us if, in the tempest and the fog, faith falters. Woe betide us if we tack, and change course, and take in canvas. For once lost, the lay of the golden land may never be recovered. The brave, bright youth becomes timid and withered, the gilded and saucy barque is a labouring, leaky hull, and at last we find ourselves, to our own scorn and the scorn of the gods, away in the grey North Sea, ignobly dredging muddy estuaries, or carrying coals from Coketown to Smokeborough.

Who would drudge with the dwarfs when he might dance with the fairies? Who, of his free choice, would plod like a brute through the miry ways of the workaday world if he could have wings for the asking? " The land of dreams is better far, above the light of the morning star."

Why, if the soul can fling the dust aside,
And naked on the air of heaven ride,
Wer't not a shame—wer't not a shame for him
In this clay carcass crippled to abide?

The great use of heroes consists in their power to lift men's souls out of the mire, to help faith live, and keep enthusiasms warm.

Do you remember what Robert Louis Stevenson says of the English admirals. He writes of Grenville's marvellous single-handed combat with the Spanish fleet—

The worth of such actions is not a thing to be decided in a quaver of sensibility or a flush of righteous common sense. The man who wished to make the ballads of his country coveted a small matter compared to what Richard Grenville accomplished. I wonder how many people have been inspired by this mad story, and how many battles have been won for England in the spirit thus engendered. . . . His work of art, his finished tragedy, is an eloquent performance ; and I contend it ought not only to enliven men of the sword as they go into battle, but send back merchant clerks with more heart and spirit to their book-keeping by double entry.

Such men as Grenville, Raleigh, and Nelson, and with them such different men as John Ball and Samuel Rutherford, bring salvation to a sordid and flaccid world ; they keep the soul clean and the heart green, their enthusiasm sounds in our sleepy ears like the blast of silver trumpets, and their faith attracts our eyes and rouses our spirit like a vision of battle banners glorious in the sun.

. . . . . .

I said above that Rutherford wrote in an age when English prose was in the making.

King James's bishops, who prepared the revised version of the Bible while Rutherford

was between his fourth and eleventh year,
and compiled the Prayer-Book, were masters
of English; so were Sidney and Raleigh; so
was Shakespeare—more than a master—a
maker of English; but the prose of these
men was chiefly of an exalted or poetic kind,
not formed to be a vehicle for quick and
easy expression of thought upon everyday
subjects. English prose did not find itself
until Dryden appeared, and did not perfect
itself for some time afterwards.

The prose of Sidney and of Raleigh at its
best was a marvellously beautiful form of
literary jewellery; but it was altogether "too
bright and good for human nature's daily
food." The prose of Shakespeare was
perfect—for his purpose. Poet's prose is
admirable—for poets. But there are few
poets, and most men must needs write at
times, and to attempt the spoken prose of
Orlando or the written prose of Milton
would be to fail contemptibly. Let us look
at the first speech of Orlando—

As I remember, Adam, it was upon this fashion :
bequeathed me by will but poor a thousand crowns,

68

and, as thou sayest, charged my brother, on his blessing, to breed me well ; and there begins my sadness. My brother Jaques he keeps at school, and report speaks goldenly of his profit : for my part, he keeps me rustically at home, or, to speak more properly, stays me here at home unkept ; for call you that keeping for a gentleman of my birth, that differs not from the stalling of an ox? His horses are bred better, for besides that they are fair with their feeding, they are taught their manage, and to that end riders dearly hired : but I, his brother, gain nothing under him but growth ; for the which his animals on his dunghills are as much bound to him as I.

That is graceful, virile, and mellifluous prose, but not suitable to the journalist or essay writer. Compare it with this from the Church Prayer-Book—

There was never anything by the wit of man so well devised, or so sure established, which in continuance of time hath not been corrupted, as among other things it may plainly appear by the Common Prayers in the Church, commonly called *Divine Service.* The first original and ground whereof if a man would search out by the ancient Fathers, he shall find that the same was not ordained but of a good purpose, and for a good advancement of godliness.

Stately and clear, but still the prose of the cloister rather than of the world. Here is a short passage from Milton—

What could a man require more from a nation so pliant and so prone to seek after knowledge? What wants there to such a towardly and pregnant soil but wise and faithful labourers to make a knowing people, a nation of prophets, of sages, and of worthies? We reckon more than five months yet to harvest; theie need not be five weeks. Had we but eyes to lift up, the fields are white already.

That is Milton in a mood of plainness. Yet the prose has a certain pomp of action. Now look at this from Dryden—

What Virgil wrote in the vigour of his age, in plenty and at ease, I have undertaken to translate in my declining years: struggling with wants, oppiessed with sickness, curbed in my genius, liable to be misconstrued in all I write.

There at last is the beginning of the new English prose. If we compare Dryden with Addison and Swift, and follow the lines of development down to De Quincey, Macaulay, Kinglake, Matthew Arnold, and Stevenson,—

a task for which I cannot afford space,—we shall not fail to see that the gain of modern prose is in its superior fluidity and plainness ; its loss, as compared with the prose of the Elizabethan masters, is the loss of melody and strength.

To-day there are some signs of decay. There is a straining after the bizarre and the "precious." Note the prose of Meredith and Mrs. Meynell. Here is a specimen of Mrs. Meynell's manner—

> To attend to a living child is to be baffled in your humour, disappointed of your pathos, and set freshly free from all the preoccupations. You cannot antici- pate him. Blackbirds, overheard year by year, do not compose the same phrases—never two *leit motifs* alike. Not the tone but the tune alters. With the uncove- nanted ways of a child you keep no tryst. They meet you at another place, after failing you where you tar- ried ; your former experiences, your documents, are at fault. You are the fellow-traveller of a bird. The bird alights, and escapes out of time to your footing.

That is pretty and ingenious, but rather strained. The form of the sentence "not the tone but the tune alters," the use of "tarried" for "waited" and "footing" for

" steps " or " footsteps " are blemishes of the
" precious " school. With all its prettiness
and skill, such laboured writing and fastidious
phrasing wearies one very soon. As a stylist
Mrs. Meynell is much admired, yet is there
not in her work some faint echo of Osric,
with his " imponed " weapons, his " carriages,
very dear to fancy, very responsive to the
hilts, and of very liberal conceit."

But J am losing sight of my goal. The
prose of Rutherford's time was, as I have
indicated, more imaginative, more poetical,
and less fluid than the prose of Dryden and
Addison. Rutherford's contemporaries were
all more or less under the influence of the
Elizabethan galaxy, as the work of Jeremy
Taylor, Sir Thomas Browne, and Milton
shows. But the need for clearer continuity
and easier movement was making itself felt,
and I think that in these directions
Rutherford was one of the most advanced.
As witness the following passage :—

Remember, when the race is ended, and the play
either won or lost, and ye are in the utmost circle and
border of time, and shall put your foot within the

march of eternity, and all your good things of this short night-dream shall seem to you like the ashes of a bleeze of thorns or straw, and your poor soul shall be crying, "Lodging, lodging, for God's sake!" then shall your soul be more glad at one of your Lord's lovely and homely smiles than if ye had the charters of three worlds for all eternity.

And this again—

The smell of Christ's wine and apples (which surpass the uptaking of dull sense) bloweth upon my soul. . . . Nay, His cross is the sweetest burden that ever I bare ; it is such a burden as wings are to a bird, or sails are to a ship, to carry me forward to my harbour.

In the qualities of picturesqueness and sweetness of phrase Rutherford's prose is of the best, and howsoever bravely, even gaily, his thick-crowding fancies may be dressed, yet the pure radiance of spiritual light shines upon and glorifies them all.

I may not quote further from this "seraphic" book. Those who love spiritual sweetness and literary grace will find them in *Selected Letters of Samuel Rutherford.* London: Oliphant Anderson & Ferrier. Price 1s., cloth.

73

A BOOK OF GAY WISDOM

JOHN SELDEN seems to have been a typical Englishman; level-headed, calm-spirited, cheerful, sincere, fond of the middle way, seeking always for the golden mean, gifted with the clearest and strongest common sense, indefatigable industry, and a saving grace of humour.

Being, as he was, a brave and outspoken gentleman, of unstained honour, deep and wide learning, and serene wisdom, he was bound to come into collision with the sainted Charles; and it will surprise no one to find that he was more than once persecuted and imprisoned by that wrong-headed and impossible king.

Selden was a great lawyer, and wrote many important books on law, the most famous being a work on the privileges of the Peers, which occupied a good deal of his time for twenty years.

He was also a member of Parliament and a powerful speaker, and used his gifts and opportunities with courage and wisdom in defence of the liberties of the people and the rights of Parliament.

Born at Salvington, near Worthing, in 1584, Selden was educated at Chichester and Oxford, and in 1602 (while Rutherford was a baby) he entered himself at Clifford's Inn. He published his great work on the Peers in 1642, was appointed Keeper of the Records in the Tower (where he had twice been a prisoner) in 1643, and was made Master of Trinity Hall, Cambridge, in 1645. Nine years later, in November 1654, he died.

Amongst his contemporaries were Shakespeare, Raleigh, Cervantes, George Chapman, Corneille, Milton, Cromwell, Hampden, Sir Thomas Browne, Beaumont and Fletcher, and Bacon. There is something quaint in the record that in 1633, when a masque of Ben Jonson's was played before Charles the First and his queen, the scenery was painted and arranged by Inigo Jones, and the dresses and properties were attended to by Lord Bacon and John Selden. What lines for a pantomime bill !

The Gorgeous and Beautiful
MASQUE
By BEN JONSON.
(*Rare Ben.*)

———

The Sumptuous and Picturesque
SCENERY
By INIGO JONES.

———

The Chaste and Elegant
COSTUMES
From the Original Designs of
LORD BACON.

———

Property Master,
JOHN SELDEN.

———

What would Crummles do with a bill like that ?

Selden died just before the Protectorate, and during the great naval war with the Dutch, when Blake and Van Tromp were fighting desperately for the empire of the

sea. Oddly enough, there is no allusion to
this war, nor to the great civil war between
Charles and the Parliament, nor to the work
of Shakespeare, Bacon, or Cervantes, in
Selden's Table Talk. Yet Selden must have
been deeply interested in all these matters.

One wonders what manner of wardrobe-
master Francis Bacon made, and whether
the sage John Selden flirted with the ladies
of the company. Doubtless he did. True,
he does not appear to have held the sex in
great esteem ; but then neither did Schopen-
hauer, and yet for all his cynicism, the
German philosopher loved at least one of
"that undersized, narrow-shouldered, broad-
hipped, and short-legged race" wiselier than
well. Therefore one would be bold to go
bail for any son of Adam in such case ; and
there is a light in Selden's eye, though he
did say of wives, "'Tis reason a man that
will have a wife should be at the charge of
her trinkets, and pay all scores she sets on
him. He that will keep a monkey 'tis fit he
should pay for the glasses he breaks." Let
us remember, too, that Selden enjoyed a

joke; and what man never made merry at woman's cost? Ungrateful dogs that we are, we must be barking.

Selden's portrait shows us a well-cut oval face, with laughter in the sparkling grey eyes, and, one would think, pleasure in the full and handsome lips. The nose is long and firm, the eyebrows broad, the dark hair curling down heavily over the high cambric collar. A face full of thought and power, a good face too, and not unmarked by care and study. He was a tall man, over six feet high, and broad shouldered, but not heavy.

For his character I must refer you to the acts of his life and the words of his contemporaries. He was fond of company, kept a plentiful table, and delighted to entertain learned and brilliant men. "I will keep myself warm and moist," said he, "as long as I live, for I shall be dry and cold when I am dead." Yet he was very temperate in eating and in drinking. And though he was "not mad enough to call himself a Puritan," he was nearer to the Puritans than to the Court in his faith and his ideals.

And now let us see what his friend Lord Clarendon said of him—

He was a person whom no character can flatter or transmit in any expressions equal to his merit and virtue. He was of such stupendous learning in all kinds, and in all languages, that a man would have thought he had been entirely conversant among books; yet his humanity, courtesy, and affability were such that he would have been thought to have been bred in the best Courts but that his good nature, charity, and delight in doing good and communicating all he knew exceeded that good breeding.

Like Montaigne, Selden won and retained the goodwill and deep respect of his country-men on both sides of the religious and political chasms which so sharply divided society in his day, and it has been well said of him that

He appears to have been regarded somewhat in the light of a valuable piece of national property, like a museum, or great public library, resorted to as a matter of course, and a matter of right in all the numerous cases in which assistance was wanted from any part of the whole compass of legal and historical learning.

The book called *Selden's Table Talk* is a collection of recollected sayings by the Rev. Richard Milward, Selden's amanuensis for many years.

It has been alleged that the utterances were tampered with by Milward, this allegation being based upon the opinion that a man of such erudition as Selden was, would not employ such homely illustrations and examples in elucidating grave and difficult questions of state and religion.

But the evidence in favour of the genuineness of the book is very strong.

In the first place, Mr. Milward declares that he carefully wrote down the sayings during a close acquaintance of twenty years.

In the second place, he publicly appealed to Selden's contemporaries and friends as to whether or not the *Table Talk* was true to Selden's conversational style and method.

In the third place, Clarendon says of Selden, " In his conversation he was the most clear discourser, and had the best faculty of making hard things easy, and of presenting them to the understanding, of any man that hath been known."

But in the excellent preface by Mr. S. W. Singer to the edition I have (Gibbings & Có., London, 2s. 6d.), there are some quotations from a parliamentary debate in which Selden took part which seem to me to put the authorship of the *Table Talk* above all question.

In this debate Selden had protested against the discussion of religious subjects in the House. In opposition Sir Harbottle Grimstone said—

That bishops are *Jure divino* is a question ; that archbishops are not *Jure divino* is out of question. Now, that bishops who are questioned whether *Jure divino* or archbishops, who out of question are not *Jure divino*, should suspend ministers that are *Jure divino*, I leave to be considered.

To this Selden replied as follows :—

That the convocation is *Jure divino* is a question ; that Parliaments are not *Jure divino* is out of question ; that religion is *Jure divino* there is no question. Now, sir, that the convocation, which is questionable whether *Jure divino*, and Parliaments, which out of question are not *Jure divino*, should meddle with religion, which questionless is *Jure divino*, I leave to your consideration.

Thereto Sir Harbottle made answer that "archbishops are not bishops," when Selden said, "*that is no otherwise true than that judges are no lawyers, and aldermen no citizens.*" In that witty and acutely logical reply we have a proof presumptive of the genuineness of Mr. Milward's report of Selden's conversation as given in the *Table Talk*.

I bought *Selden's Table Talk* a couple of years since, on the strength of his reputation. I had read many allusions to it as an excellent book, and when in one of my rambles in Booksellers' Row I saw a nicely bound copy at a reasonable price I treated myself, and went home well pleased with my treasure.

I put Selden in the bank—that is to say, I tucked him cosily by amongst the best of good company, there to rest until some "rainy day," when an unread good book should be the one thing needful.

Some months later the day came. I was rearranging my books, and while stooping to pick up a fallen volume, the lumbago gripped me by the small of the back, and I rolled, a helpless bundle, on the floor. There I remained for a full week, on a mattress, like Bill Barley "on the broad of his back, by the Lord," to understudy Mark Tapley and repent of my sins.

Midmost of my involuntary vigil I made my first acquaintance with Selden. It was late one night, and all the house asleep. I had propped myself up in a sitting posture against my desk, packed in with pillows, and with a good fire burning on my port broadside, and having got my pipe well going, I began to turn the leaves of my new companion.

Imagine my dismay as I ran my eye over the headings of the short articles and paragraphs into which the little book is divided : "Abbeys, Priories," "Baptism," "Bible, Scripture," "Bishops before the Parliament," "Canon Law," "Ceremony," "High Commission," "House of Commons,"

83

"Holy Days," "Imperial Constitutions," "Imprisonment." My face fell. I sighed. Here had I invited a cheerful gossip to entertain me, and behold a frosty pedant full of dry-as-dust tattle about religion and law. I should have laid the book down then and there, but to crawl across the room for another would have been no joke, and I could not sleep for the grinding twinges of rheumatism in my knee. Very listlessly, and in no gracious mood, I began to read—

The unwillingness of the monks to part with their land will fall out to be just nothing, because they are yielded up to the king by a supreme hand, viz. a Parliament. If a king conquer another country the people are loth to lose their lands; yet no divine will deny but the king may give them to whom he please. If a Parliament make a law concerning leather, or any other commodity, you and I, for example, are Parliament men; perhaps in respect to our own private interests we are against it; yet the major part conclude it; we are then involved, and the law is good.

It was a wild night. The wind was howling round the chimneys, the sleet hissed upon the window panes, the blaze chuckled and whispered in the grate. I glanced back at the preface. Selden died in 1654, yet how near he seemed. I could almost imagine the tones of his voice, the light in his eye. He kept a good table, and much good company. Perhaps Clarendon, Bacon, Cotton, and other famous men sat at his board as he spoke of the poor monks and their objections. Fancy the scene. The wainscoted room, the soft light of candles, the golden canary in the old decanters, and Selden, his oval face animated, his fine white hand playing with his silver cup, goes on talking—

When the founders of the abbeys laid a curse upon those that should take away those lands, I would fain know what power they had to curse me. 'Tis not the curses that come from the poor, or from anybody, that hurt me, because they come from them, but because I do something ill against them that deserves God should curse me for it. On the other side, 'tis not a man's blessing me that makes me blessed; he only declares me to be so, and if I do well I shall be blessed, whether any bless me or not.

This was not the kind of thing I had feared from the headings. This was bright talk, clear thought, cheerful, illuminating, and not unpleasing to a Socialist. I drew my pipe into a good humour, settled my pillows, and read the whole book straight through.

The quiet humour of Selden, the homeliness and aptness of his illustrations, his remarkable gift for " making hard things easy," pleased and surprised me. Surely nowhere could one find such shrewd, terse, and vivid sermons upon texts so unpromising. Thus he speaks upon " Equity "—

Equity is a roguish thing; for law we have a measure, know what to trust to. Equity is according to the conscience of him that is Chancellor, and as that is larger or narrower, so is equity. 'Tis all one as if they should make the standard for the measure we call a foot, a Chancellor's foot. What an uncertain measure would this be. One Chancellor has a long foot, another a short foot, a third an indifferent foot. 'Tis the same thing in the Chancellor's conscience.

How clearly expressed is that, how quaintly put, and what a strong smack of personality and character it conveys. One recognises at once not only the power of a correct and lucid thinker, but also the native humour and whim of an original and visibly honest man. Let us hear the same oracle on learning—

No man is the wiser for his learning : it may administer matter to work in, or objects to work upon ; but wit and wisdom are born with a man.

Selden was himself a learned man ; but his wit and wisdom were born with him, and his learning had not blunted the one nor obscured the other—

. . . We measure the goodness of God from ourselves ; we measure His goodness, His justice, His wisdom, by something we call just, good, or wise in ourselves ; and in so doing we judge proportionately to the country fellow in the play who said if he were a king he would live like a lord, and have peas and bacon every day, and a whip that cried slash.

Such homely illustrations are all the more forcible from their unexpectedness. One does not anticipate the country bumpkin and his whip that cries slash in an argument about the wisdom of Providence.

'Tis ridiculous to say the tithes are God's part, and therefore the clergy must have them. Why, so they are if the layman has them. 'Tis as if one of my Lady Kent's maids should be sweeping this room, and another of them should come and take away the broom, and tell her for a reason she should part with it, "'tis my lady's broom"; as if it were not my lady's broom which of them soever had it.

Selden was master of the art of hitting the right nail on the head. He does not boggle about his work, but gets it done out of hand with few strokes and deft.

Prayer should be short, without giving God Almighty reasons why He should grant this or that. He knows best what is good for us. If your boy should ask you a suit of clothes, and give you reasons, "otherwise he cannot wait upon you, he cannot go abroad but he will discredit you," would you endure it? You know it better than he; let him ask a suit of clothes.

All through the book we find the like apt and humble illustrations, the same shrewdness and good common sense—

Religion is like the fashion; one man wears his doublet slashed, another laced, another plain, but every man has a doublet. So every man has his religion: we differ about the trimming.

88

The art of making hard things easy is as rare as it is useful. There is hardly a problem of life that might not be made clear and simple to the general mind had we a man with wit and sagacity enough for the task. The "dismal science" is sorely in need of a Selden.

WILLIAM MORRIS: SONG-SMITH

ARTEMUS WARD'S anecdote of the drummer always tickled me on the laughing strings. "There was a man in New South Wales," he said eagerly, "who hadn't a tooth in his head." Here he paused, and added in serious tones, "and yet that man could beat a drum as well as anybody."

Well, I should say of William Morris, "There is not one famous man in a thousand with so many shining talents as Morris had, and yet he could not beat a drum at all." A strong thinker, a brilliant designer, a master craftsman, a virile romancer, and a noble poet, Morris was; but he did not advertise. He seemed, like our dear old impossible Morrison Davidson, to suppose that when an author had written a good book he had done his whole duty. Any journalist could have told him that the booming of the work was quite as important as its conception and execution. But no journalist did tell him this; perhaps because Morris had such peculiar views and such a volcanic reputation. The consequence is that, although the name of William Morris is almost as well known as the names of Dan Leno and Sir Wilfrid Lawson, his books are by no means popular.

Outside Socialist ranks he is better known as a maker of wallpaper than as a poet. Inside Socialist ranks his writings are not widely read. The pamphlets, *News from Nowhere*, *Poems by the Way*, and *A Dream of John Ball*, are familiar; but how many have read *The Defence of Guenevere*, *The Roots of the Mountains*, and *The Earthly Paradise?* True, the title of the latter book is almost as commonly known as if it were the name of a new beef-tea. So are the titles of the *Faerie Queene* and *Paradise Lost*, of *The Tale of a Tub* and *Leaves of Grass*; but these works are not popular in the sense in which *The Sorrows of Satan* and *The Seven Seas* are popular.

A list of William Morris's books would come as a surprise, even to many Socialists who read. Let me jot them down as I remember them.

There are the translations of the *Æneid* and the *Odyssey* (these I have never even seen). There are—

The Earthly Paradise.
The Defence of Guenevere.
The Life and Death of Jason.
The Story of Sigurd the Volsung.
Poems by the Way.
Signs of Change.
The Roots of the Mountains.
The House of the Wolfings.
The Well at the World's End.
News from Nowhere.
The Story of the Glittering Plain.
A Dream of John Ball.
The Sundering Flood.
The Water of the Wondrous Isle.
The Wood Beyond the World,

and some pamphlets on art and Socialism. Except the two translations and *The Story of Sigurd* I have read all the books above named. There are eight prose romances, including *News from Nowhere*, and five books of poems. I should place *The Defence of Guenevere* and parts of *The Earthly Paradise* highest of all the poetry, and *A Dream of John Ball* and *The Roots of the Mountains* first of all the prose, although in its own way, as a picture of an ideal common-wealth, *News from Nowhere* is a very beautiful and convincing piece of work.

In the interests of the reading public, and apart from the interests of humanity and art, the best of Morris's work ought to be more widely known. Cheap editions of *News from Nowhere* and *A Dream of John Ball* may be had; but *The Roots of the Mountains* is only published at 8s., *The Earthly Paradise* at 7s. 6d., and *The Defence of Guenevere* at 6s. This is not as it should be. Only the well-to-do reader, who *will* have books, or the literary man who *must* have them, can give such prices. Cheaper editions would help the public, and pay the publishers well.

Of all Morris's work, the two books I most love are *The Defence of Guenevere* and

93

A Dream of John Ball. These I hold to be his masterpieces in poetry and prose.

I wish first of all to say a little about *The Defence of Guenevere* and some of the other poems, because I feel that as a poet William Morris has not received his full meed of honour.

Morris was always virile. His romances are full of fighting, and his poetry is sensuous, passionate, rich in colour, deep in feeling, alive with quick warm pulses beating strongly. The "Idle Singer of an Empty Day" never sang idly, and not often quietly. But his strength is always within measure, and in his most lambent and fervid poems his artistic restraint is never relaxed. Of *The Earthly Paradise* I shall say very little. As a long-sustained work it is remarkably free from blemishes, and if at times it sinks to pedestrian levels, it is rich in sunny flights and gushes of spontaneous song. Few have surpassed Morris in the difficult art of quick and graceful narrative in verse. Not always felicitous as to his versification, he was, even in that department, of the masters,

94

at his best, and he is at his best very
frequently in *The Earthly Paradise.* As
witness this well-known verse—

Dreamer of dreams, born out of my due time,
　Why should I strive to set the crooked straight?
Let it suffice me that my murmuring rhyme
　Beats with light wing against the ivory gate,
　Telling a tale not too importunate
　　To those who in the sleepy region stay,
　　Lulled by the singer of an empty day.

But the most lovely and perfect little lyric
Morris ever wrote, and one of the most
perfect and sweet in the language, is the
duet in "Ogier the Dane"—

　　In the white-flowered hawthorn brake,
　　Love, be merry for my sake ;
　　Twine the blossoms in my hair,
　　Kiss me where I am most fair—
　　Kiss me, love, for who knoweth
　　What thing cometh after death ?

　　Nay, the garlanded gold hair
　　Hides thee where thou art most fair ;
　　Hides the rose-tinged hills of snow—
　　Ah, sweet love, I have thee now !
　　Kiss me, love, for who knoweth
　　What thing cometh after death ?

Weep, O love, the days that flit,
  Now, while I can feel thy breath ;
Then may I remember it
  Sad and old, and near my death.
Kiss me, love, for who knoweth
What thing cometh after death ?

That has always seemed to me one of the
few lyrics worthy to rank with the wild-bird,
open-air, merrie English songs of Shakespeare.

Note now the splendour and warm colour-
ing in this description of "The House of
Venus." It alway sounds to me as though it
belonged by right to the *Faerie Queene*—

Dusky and dim, though rich with gems and gold,
The House of Venus was ; high in the dome
The burning sunlight you could now behold,
From nowhere else the light of day might come,
To shame the Shame-faced Mother's lovely home ;
A long way off the shrine, the fresh sea breeze,
Now just arising, brushed the myrtle trees.

Morris is not always at that height in *The
Earthly Paradise* ; but when we open *The
Defence of Guenevere* we find him in the full

tide of his strength, and the firm and subtle mastery of his passion and his cunning.

There are two of the Arthurian legends treated in this book, which contains, besides several other fine poems, notably "Sir Peter Harpden's End" and "The Haystack in the Floods."

The first poem (which gives the title to the book) is "The Defence of Guenevere." It presents to us King Arthur's queen, standing at bay before the accusing knights, headed by the beetle-browed Sir Gauwaine.

But, knowing now that they would have her
    speak,
She threw her wet hair backward from her brow,
Her hand close to her mouth, touching her cheek,
As though she had had there a shameful blow,
And feeling it shameful to feel aught but shame
All through her heart, yet felt her cheek burned so,
She must a little touch it; like one lame
She walked away from Gauwaine, with her head
Still lifted up, and in her cheek of flame
The tears dried quick; . . .

Before her the knights stand, silent, listening; not once do they speak all through her passionate monologue. And what a speech

G   97

hers is, now swift with eagerness, now broken with emotion, by turns ecstatic, pleading or defiant—as it is dominated by the queen's pride, the woman's weakness, or the delirious, fearless joy of the lover. Nowhere, that I can remember, has that strange human story of the struggle between the new love and the old been rendered with such tender strength and clear but sympathetic insight. Guenevere's allegory of the angel with the two cloths, offering the bewildered mortal choice between heaven and hell, is used with sure skill; and her denial of the gross fact, repeated passionately, is most dramatic.

Nevertheless you, O Sir Gauwaine, lie,
Whatever may have happened through these years,
God knows I speak the truth, saying that you lie.

The whole scene is given with strong dramatic power, and is so vividly graphic that we can hear the queen's voice rise to "a windy shriek in all men's ears," and then fall low, as "her great eyes again began to fill," and we can see the armed knights with glum faces, and the queen at bay as

She stood, and seemed to think, and wrung her
    hair,
Spoke out at last with no more trace of shame,
With passionate twisting of her body there.

She speaks out indeed, telling how Launcelot came, and how the choice between heaven
and hell was forced upon her, dizzied as she
was betwixt the wine-sweet temptation and
the memories "belonging to the time ere I
was bought by Arthur's great name and his
little love." Here is her story of Launcelot's
advent—

It chanced upon a day that Launcelot came
To dwell at Arthur's court; at Christmas-time
This happened; when the heralds sung his name,

Son of King Ban of Benwick, seemed to chime
Along with all the bells that rang that day
O'er the white roofs, with little change of rhyme.

Christmas and whitened Winter passed away,
And over me the April sunshine came,
Made very awful with black hail-clouds. Yea,

And in Summer I grew white with flame,
And bowed my head down—Autumn and the sick
Sure knowledge things would never be the same,

However often Spring might be most thick
Of blossoms and buds, smote on me, and I grew
Careless of most things, let the clock tick, tick,

To my unhappy pulse, that beat right through
My eager body; while I laughed out loud,
And let my lips curl up at false or true.

The same high level of restrained passion, of sure insight, and artistic excellence is preserved throughout the entire poem; through the queen's scornful denunciation of Mellyagraunce, her burning eulogy of Launcelot, her touching appeal to Gauwaine—

Do I not see how God's dear pity creeps
All through your frame, and trembles in your
    mouth?
Remember in what grave your mother sleeps,—

on to the imaginative beauty of the garden scene, and the lurid story of the combat, with "a spurt of blood on the hot land," until—

"All I have said is truth, by Christ's dear tears."
She would not speak another word, but stood.
Turn'd sideways, listening, like a man who hears

His brother's trumpet sounding through the wood
Of his foe's lances——

It is a noble poem. Compare it, and its companion, "At Arthur's Tomb," with Tennyson's "Idylls of the King," and the real grandeur of the genius of William Morris will be instantly apparent.

The whole of "The Scene at Arthur's Tomb" is intensely dramatic, and the poetical beauty and ringing power of the dialogue are above criticism. Here are the final words with which the heartbroken queen breaks down the desire and slays the hope of the man she loves—

"Banner of Arthur—with black-bended shield.

"Sinister-wise across the fair gold ground,
Here let me tell you what a knight you are,
O sword and shield of Arthur! You are found
A crooked sword, I think, that leaves a scar

"On the bearer's arm, so he thinks it straight,
Twisted Malay's creese beautiful blue-grey,
Poisoned with sweet fruit, as he found too late,
My husband Arthur, on some bitter day;

"O sickle cutting hemlock the day long!
That husbandman across his shoulder hangs,
And going homeward, about evensong,
Dies the next morning, struck through by the fangs;

"Banner, and sword, and shield, you dare not
    pray to die,
Lest Arthur meet you in the other world,
And, knowing who you are, he pass you by,
Taking short turns that he may watch you curled

"Body and face and limbs in agony,
Lest he weep presently and go away,
Saying, 'I loved him once,' with a sad sigh—
Now I have slain him, Lord, let me go too, I pray."

That is such poetry that one must needs regret that its author did not go deeper in the Mallory mine and fashion of its metal more such cups of gold, tall, graceful, carved with curious beauty, and filled with the red wine that runs warm in the quick hearts of real women and real men.

I should like to quote from "Sir Peter Harpden's End," but can hardly tell where to begin or to leave off; suppose I take some lines near the end, where the lady, dreaming of her absent lover, hears the trumpet of the herald who comes to tell her of his shameful death. The dialogue following this is dramatic, and painfully pathetic, but it is too long to quote entire, and would be spoilt

by any omissions. Thus, then, the lady
communes with her own anxious soul—

> I cannot bear the noisy
> And lighted street out there, with this thought
>   alive,
> Like any curling snake within my brain ;
> Let me just hide my head within these soft,
> Deep cushions, there to try and think it out.
>
> I cannot hear much noise now, and I think
> That I shall go to sleep : it all sounds dim
> And faint, and I shall soon forget most things ;
> Yea, almost that I am alive and here ;
> It goes slow, comes slow, like a big mill-wheel
> On some broad stream, with long green weeds
>   asway,
> And soft and slow it rises and it falls,
> Still going onward.
>
> Lying so, one kiss,
> And I should be in Avalon asleep,
> Among the poppies and the yellow flowers ;
> And they should brush my cheek, my hair being
>   spread
> Far out among the stems ; soft mice and small
> Eating and creeping all about my feet,
> Red shod and tired ; and the flies should come
> Creeping o'er my broad eyelids unafraid ;
> And there should be a noise of water going,

Clear blue, fresh water breaking on the slates,
Likewise the flies should creep—God's eyes! God
   help,
A trumpet? I will run fast, leap adown
The slippery sea stairs where the crabs fight.

        Ah!
I was half dreaming, but the trumpet's true,
He stops here at our house. The Clisson Arms?
Ah, now for news. But I must hold my heart,
And be quite gentle till he is gone out,
And afterwards—but he is still alive,
He must be still alive.

   I suppose it is greedy to ask for more, and ungracious to complain. But I'd give up all the prose romances of William Morris, with the sole exception of *John Ball*, for one other book of poems such as are in this volume of two hundred and forty-eight small pages. One more quotation, and I will put the good book down. It is from "The Haystack in the Floods," and gives a wonderful description of a ride in the rain; the whole atmosphere, natural and dramatic, is magnificently rendered—

     Had she come all the way for this,
     To part at last without a kiss?

·104

Yea, had she borne the dirt and rain
That her own eyes might see him slain
Beside the haystack in the floods?

Along the dripping leafless woods,
The stirrup touching either shoe,
She rode astride as troopers do ;
With kirtle kilted to her knee,
To which the mud splashed wretchedly ;
And the wet dripped from every tree
Upon her head and heavy hair,
And on her eyelids broad and fair ;
The tears and rain ran down her face.

.   .   .   .   .   .

Ah me, she had but little ease ;
And, often for pure doubt and dread,
She sobbed, made giddy in the head
By the swift riding, while, for cold,
Her slender fingers scarce could hold
The wet reins ; yea, and scarcely too,
She felt the foot within her shoe
Against the stirrup, and all for this,
To part at last without a kiss
Beside the haystack in the floods.

William Morris always spoke of himself
modestly as a "song-smith"; but he was
more than any song-smith, he was a poet,
and his fire was divine.

"A DREAM OF JOHN BALL"

I SHOULD call *A Dream of John Ball* the best of William Morris's prose romances. The style is easier, the aim is higher, the story is more compact, and the artist's gift of selection has been more skilfully exercised than in any other prose work from the same pen. The excellences of the book are the excellences of Morris's other prose tales, but somewhat finer. The author's faculty of picturesqueness is here at its best. The faces and costumes of the men and women are visible to us : the scene at the cross, the battle at the township's end, the dead laid out in the church, are all so graphically painted,—the grouping so artistic, the background so cunningly laid in—that they remain in the memory as things seen. Which of us forgets Will Green's daughter, as she comes up with the arrows? Here we have the green meadows and the sinking sun, the billmen massed in a sheltered angle, the bowmen in line behind the hedges. Green has taken off his belts, hung his coat upon a tree, and stuck a score of arrows into the turf beside him. "Most of the bowmen within sight doing the like." Then the artist, with a few sure touches, lays in the picture—

As I glanced toward the houses I saw three or four bright figures moving through the orchards, and presently noticed that they were women, all clad more or less like the girl in the Rose, except that two of them wore white coifs on their heads. Their errand was clear, for each carried a bundle of arrows under her arm.

One of them came straight up to Will Green, and I could see at once that she was his daughter. She was tall and strongly made, with black hair like her father, somewhat comely, but no great beauty ; but as they met, her eyes smiled even more than her mouth, and made her face look very sweet and kind, and the smile was answered back in a way so quaintly like to her father's face, that I too smiled for good will and pleasure.

The fighting, of course, is perfectly

described.   Morris, with all his love of peace and beauty, was too much of a Viking not to relish a feast of blows.   Like gentle Toby Shandy, he loves brave faces and white steel. Read " The End of Peter Harpden," Queen Guenevere's account of the death of Mellyagraunce, the great battle between the dark men and the true men in *The Roots of the Mountains*, the rout of the Roman legion in *The Wolfings*, and see with what zest Morris goes into the fray. Indeed, I know few writers so fond of battle-pieces, or so good at painting them.   The great battle in *The Roots of the Mountains* is a masterpiece, for Morris had the eye of a general as well as the touch of an artist ; and yet I prefer this fight at the town's end in *John Ball* to all others of Morris's make.   It is so clear, so graphic, so concise, and told with such fine artistic reserve.

Morris's limitations are, chiefly, a weakness of characterisation and an almost painful absence of humour.   The characters in *John Ball* are little more than outlines. The faces and the costumes are skilfully

done, but the men and women are only men
and women, they have little personality.
The figure of John Ball himself is only a
figure. Most of the other characters are
dream figures. Note the scene in the ale-
house. The picture is perfect, but there is
little character shown, and no humour.
Imagine what Shakespeare or Scott would
have made of that company, and it is at
once evident that Morris has no eye for
character. Character as character does not
seem to have appealed to him. The "Mad
Priest" gives his message, and performs
certain acts, but there is nothing but his gown
and his name to distinguish him from the
crowd of other men. They are all brave,
honest, bluff, and of direct and severe speech.
John Ball, Will Green, and the rest, are all
of a colour. Morris has given to no one of
them any of those personal traits, mannerisms,
expressions, twists of thought and surprises of
humour which express character. Contrast
John Ball as drawn by Morris with Fra
Lippo Lippi as drawn by Browning. In all
Morris's prose stories I can remember no

striking character. This is due, I believe, to lack of humour. Morris concerned himself chiefly with the picture and the moral; the humours of a situation or a character seem always to have eluded him. In *John Ball* there is a smile at the lawyer's attempt to read the Riot Act of the period, but it is a very quiet smile. And never, so far as I am aware, in this book or in any other, has William Morris woke us into laughter.

Nevertheless *A Dream of John Ball* is a beautiful piece of work, and one to be grateful for, and some readers may think that in such a dreamy, poetical, and elevated work laughter would be as incongruous as in a church. For my part, I like an occasional smile, and such a character as the archer uncle of Quentin Durward would be very welcome to me in Morris's masterpiece.

Morris's version of John Ball's speech at the cross is very beautiful. How much of the speech is historical and how much original I cannot say, but many of the finest passages are absent from the speech as it stands in Green's *Short History*. For instance, "fellowship is heaven, and lack of fellowship is hell," is in Morris but not in Green, and I am constrained to think that Ball's eloquence at the cross owes a very great deal to William Morris, the Socialist poet. John Ball, as "reported" in Green's History, speaks as follows :—

Good people, things will never go well in England so long as goods be not in common, and so long as there be villains and gentlemen. By what right are they whom we call lords greater folk than we? On what grounds do they deserve it? Why do they hold us in serfage, if we all come of the same father and mother, of Adam and Eve? How can they say or prove that they are better than we, if it be not that they make us gain for them by our toil what they spend in their pride?

They are clothed in velvet and warm in their furs and their ermines, while we are covered with rags. They have wine and spices and fair bread; and we oat cake and straw, and water to drink. They have leisure and fine houses, and we have pain and labour, the rain, and the wind in the fields. And yet it is of us and our toil that these men hold their state.

Green's authority for that speech I cannot give. Did John Ball write his sermons? If he did not, how were they so accurately reported in a day when there were no papers and no shorthand writers?

Let us return to William Morris. The chief delight of *John Ball* for me lies in the delicate beauty of the pictures. The new church, with the white stone dust still upon the grass, the interior of the drinking room at the Rose, the figures of the yeomen returning from practice at the butts, all these are perfect. Here, for example, is a quick sketch of Ball at the cross—

He went slowly up the steps of the cross, and stood at the top with one hand laid on the shaft, and shout upon shout broke forth from the throng. When the shouting died away into a silence of the human voices, the bells were still quietly chiming with that far-away voice of theirs, and the long-winged dusky swifts, by no means scared by the concourse, swung round about the cross with their wild squeals; and the man stood still for a time eyeing the throng.

Magnificent, also, is Morris's account of the changing moods and wavering emotions of the crowd under the sway of John Ball's eloquence, and very striking are Morris's own reflections in the pauses of the speech—

But while I pondered all these things, and how men fight and lose the battle, and the thing that they fought for comes about in spite of their defeat, and when it comes turns out to be not what they meant, and other men have to fight for what they meant under another name—while I pondered all this, John Ball began to speak again in the same soft and clear voice with which he had left off.

The long conversation between Morris and Ball is rather sad, and for that reason, sadness being cheaper in this world than pleasure, I seldom read it; but the conclusion, where the priest takes leave of Morris, is excellent, for therein speaks the brave spirit of the Kelmscott poet and hero. Ball says—

Now, brother, I say farewell; for now verily hath the Day of the Earth come, and thou and I are lonely to each other again; thou hast been a dream to me as I to thee, and sorry and glad have we made each other, as tales of old time and the longing of times to come shall ever make men to be. I go to life and to death, and leave thee; and scarce do I know whether to wish thee some dream of the days beyond thine to tell what shall be, as thou hast told me, for I

H 113

know not if that shall help or hinder thee; but since we have been kind and very friends, I will not leave thee without a wish of goodwill, so at least I wish thee what thou thyself wishest for thyself, and that is hopeful strife, and blameless peace, which is to say in one word, life. Farewell, friend.

So departs John Ball, and after him now has gone William Morris. I wonder where they go to, all these good men. I wonder will Morris meet Ball, and if so whether he will find him all he is represented to be in this wonderful book. I wonder whether the men of Jack Straw's legions were *quite* such good fellows as Morris has painted them, whether they were not, like Katisha, "a little teeny bit ferocious," whether they did not find as much fun as justice in the hanging of a scrivener, whether their sports were not rather brutal, their speech rather bestial, their minds rather dark and cruel from long years of wallowing in ignorance and superstition. At anyrate, we know that their "betters" were little more than savages: men treacherous, violent, and merciless; and we can feel as glad as Morris felt when Will Green's arrows sped straight, and when the hireling men of rapine bit the dust in the hand play. And we can rejoice with Morris that the honest historian, Green, ferreted out the truth about the peasant revolt, and cleared the people's memory from the slanders which class prejudice had heaped upon it. Brave soldiers and clever bowmen there were in those days we know, for was it not soon after Crecy? And we may well thank William Morris for having brought these men so vividly before us, and for having retold a gallant old story so beautifully, and given us such lovely pictures of Old England and its people—even if the scenes and characters are brought before us coloured by the glamour of a dream.

There is a very nice pocket edition of *John Ball* in cloth at 1s. 6d., published by Reeves & Turner. This volume also includes that literary gem, " A King's Lesson."

OF GRAPHIC WRITING

THERE appear to be two great schools of graphic writing—

    1. The figurative.
    2. The literal.

The first is most used in Eastern literature. The second, which is the usual form of modern descriptive writing, may be subdivided into three styles—

    1. The severely literal.
    2. The florid.
    3. The imaginative.

The figurative school appeals to the imagination. The purely literal appeals to the memory. The florid and the imaginative appeal to the memory, to the senses, and to the imagination. Of course these divisions are arbitrary, and, equally of course, it will be found that most writers occasionally mix the various styles together. Ruskin and Carlyle, for instance, use literal and figurative separately and in combination.

Examples of figurative writing abound in the Bible, and in the Persian, Chinese, Arabic, and Sanscrit literature. A familiar instance is the description of the battle-horse in Job—

His neck is clothed with thunder. The glory of his nostrils is terrible. He swalloweth the ground with fierceness and rage. He smelleth the battle afar off.

This tells us nothing about the horse except that he is fierce and eager. Yet it conveys a more vivid *idea* of a horse than the scientific " definition " by the boy Bitzer, in *Hard Times*—

Quadruped, Graminivorous. Forty teeth, namely, twenty-four grinders, four eye teeth, and twelve incisive. Sheds coat in the spring : in marshy countries sheds hoofs, too. Hoofs hard, but requiring to be shod with iron. Age known by marks in mouth.

Boy Bitzer, I suppose, would describe his quadruped as " uttering a shrill noise, called neighing, during the progress of hostilities."

117

Job's horse "Shouts ha! ha! with the trumpets, the thunders of the captains, and the shouting, and laughs at the shaking of the spear."

Shakespeare, not having the advantage of the Gradgrind "system," goes nearer to Job than to Bitzer, and makes the Dauphin, in *Henry V.*, describe his charger thus—

When I bestride him I soar; I am a hawk. He trots the air; the earth sings when he touches it. The basest horn of his hoof is more musical than the pipe of Hermes. He's of the colour of the nutmeg, and of the heat of the ginger. It is a beast for Perseus; he is pure air and fire, and the dull elements of earth and water never appear in him but only in patient stillness while his rider mounts him. He is indeed a horse, and all other jades you may call beasts. It is the prince of palfreys. His neigh is like the bidding of a monarch, and his countenance enforces homage.

That long eulogy tells us nothing about the horse, except that he is a bay of great mettle and lightness; yet an imaginative reader can fairly hear the creature neigh, and see him prance and curvet, and arch his glossy neck.

· Let us now take examples of the purely literal style of description. Here is one from Æschylus, describing the advance of the Argives against Thebes—

For already the host of the Argives, hard at hand, armed *cap-à-pie,* is in motion, is speeding onward, and white foam is staining the plain with its drippings from the lungs of their chargers. . . . The army is let loose, having quitted its camp, a mighty mounted host, is streaming hitherward in advance. The dust appearing high in the air convinces me, a voiceless true messenger ; the noise of the clatter of their hoofs upon the plain reaching even to our couches, approaches my ears, is wafted on, and is rumbling like a resistless torrent lashing the mountain side. Alas, alas ! oh, Gods and Goddesses, avert the rising horror ; the white-bucklered, well-appointed host is rushing on.

Here the speaker describes just what he sees—the champing steeds, the white bucklers, the rising dust, the clatter of many hoofs. The facts are nowhere coloured by fancy. Even the comparisons are in measure. The rumble of the hoofs *is* like the roar of a torrent. There is no hyperbole, no metaphor. An Eastern writer would have said, "the Earth is risen up in a cloud of dust into the firmament, and the everlasting hills are shaken with the thunder of the horses."

See, for instance, Solomon's palanquin, with its "Floor of gold inlaid with love," or this—

Who is it that looketh forth as the morning; fair as the moon, clear as the sun, terrible as an army with banners?

I take my second example of the literal style from Erckmann and Chatrian's *Conscript.* It describes the breaking of a French square by Prussian Hussars—

I don't know how it happened; but there they were, swerving right and left, and bending down from their little horses to sabre us without mercy. We thrust at them with our bayonets, and shouted, and they fired pistols at us; it was a terrible time. All my life long I shall remember the pale faces, with the long moustaches, drawn back behind the ears, and the little shakos strapped tight under the chin, with the horses neighing and rearing over heaps of dead and wounded.

How simple. The description is accurate enough, and moderate enough for police-court evidence; but how vivid; what art in the arrangement and drawing of the picture.

Do you remember Thackeray's gambling scene in *Catherine?*

The dice went rattling on, the candles were burning dim, with great long wicks.

"Seven's the main," cried the Count. "Four. Three to two against the caster."

"Ponies," said the Warwickshire Squire.

Rattle, rattle, rattle, rattle, clatter, *nine.* Clap, clap, clap, clap, *eleven.* Clutter, clutter, clutter, clutter, "Seven it is," says the Warwickshire Squire.

How perfectly the writer suggests the sound of the dice. And it is so hard to suggest sound. I once stood for an hour trying to translate the toll of a big bell into syllables. "Clang" is not right, neither is "Kling Clang," nor "Ding dong." The nearest I could get was "Hlang a *lang, Hlang* a langle angle angle *angg.*" So with the sound of marching feet on gravel. "Crunch" is not right ; cranch is better. A very clever bit of sound-writing is Rudyard Kipling's "Spitting crack" of a screw cannon at billiards.

Here is a bit of literal landscape by Gilbert White—

Among the singularities of this place, the two rocky hollow lanes, the one to Alton, and the other to the forest, deserve our attention. These roads running through the malm lands, are by the traffic of all ages, and the fretting of water, worn down through the first stratum of our freestone, and partly through the second ; so that they look more like watercourses than roads, and are bedded with naked rag for furlongs together. In many places they are reduced sixteen or eighteen feet beneath the level of the fields ; and after floods, and in frosts, exhibit very grotesque and wild appearances, from the tangled roots that are twisted among the strata, and from the torrents rushing down their broken sides ; and especially when these cascades are frozen into icicles, hanging in all the fanciful shapes of frostwork.

The difference between this and the Frenchmen's battle-piece above, is the difference between original painting and sketching from Nature. White does not attempt a picture. He is writing a letter to a friend, and desires to give him an accurate account of these "rugged, gloomy scenes." His picture is graphic because it is truthful, and vivid because it is simple. The Frenchmen set to work to paint for effect, and arranged their lights and shadows with masterly skill. White simply drew what he saw. He had acquired the habit of precision, and he who draws with fidelity from Nature is bound to make effective pictures, for Nature is always effective.

As a confirmation of this view, take a few lines from Walt Whitman about Brooklyn ferry—

I, too, many and many a time crossed the river of old; watched the twelfth-month sea-gulls, saw them high in the air, floating with motionless wings oscillating their bodies,

Saw how the glistening yellow lit up parts of their bodies, leaving the rest in strong shadow,

Saw the slow wheeling circles, and the gradual edging towards the south,

Saw the reflection of the summer sky in the water,

Had my eyes dazzled by the shimmering track of beams,

Looked at the fine centrifugal spokes of light round the shape of my head in the sunlit water,

Looked on the haze on the hills southward and south-westward,

Looked on the vapour as it flew in fleeces tinged with violet.

That is a perfect picture, but it is scrupulously faithful. The whole thing is as frank and simple as an auctioneer's catalogue, yet full of a wonderful feeling of the swimming

123

river, and the dancing light-sparkles, and
the wavering cloud reflections, and the great
gulls, sailing, sailing.

Of the florid style: here is an example
from *Othello*—

Methinks the wind has spoke aloud at land ;
A fuller blast ne'er shook our battlements ;
If it hath ruffianed so upon the sea
What ribs of oak, when mountains melt upon them,
Can hold the mortise? . . .
For do but stand upon the foaming shore,
The chidden billow seems to pelt the clouds ;
The wind-shaked surge, with high and monstrous
    mane,
Seems to cast water on the burning bear,
And quench the guards of the ever fixed pole.

Here is another, from Ruskin : *Modern
Painters*—

But as I climbed the long slope of the Alban
Mount, the storm swept finally to the north, and the
noble outline of the domes of Albans, and the graceful darkness of its ilex grove, rose against pure
streaks of alternate blue and amber ; the upper sky
gradually flushing through the last fragments of
rain-cloud in deep palpitating azure, half ether and
half dew. The noonday sun came slanting down

the rocky slopes of La Riccia, and their masses of entangled and tall foliage, whose autumnal tints were mixed with the wet verdure of a thousand evergreens, were penetrated with it as with rain. I cannot call it colour, it was conflagration.

That is a pure example of the florid style. By the florid style I mean the descriptive style which embellishes its subject with poetical similes and graces of language. If we imagine how Walt Whitman or Gilbert White would describe that scene in the Campagna we shall readily perceive the difference betwixt the florid and the plain.

In the imaginative style of description the subject is illuminated with *fanciful* or *imaginative* similes and *suggestive* language. Read the description given by Dickens of a burning château, in the *Tale of Two Cities*—

Presently the château began to make itself *strangely visible* by some light of its own, *as though it were growing luminous*. Then a flickering streak played behind the architecture of the front, picking out transparent places, and showing where balustrades, arches, and windows were. Then it soared higher, and grew broader and brighter. Soon, from a score of the great windows, flames burst forth, *and the stone faces, awakened*, stared out of the fire.

The château was left to itself to flame and burn. In the roaring and raging of the conflagration, *a red-hot wind, driving straight from the infernal regions*, seemed to be *blowing the edifice away*. With the rising and falling of the blaze the stone faces showed *as if they were in torment*. When great masses of stone and timber fell, the face with the two dints in the nose became obscured, anon *struggled out of the smoke again*, as if it were the face of the cruel Marquis *burning at the stake and contending with the fire*.

How the picture is lighted up by these flashes of fancy. Take another imaginative piece of description, from Carlyle's *French Revolution*—

Unhappy friends, the tocsin does yield, has yielded! Lo ye, how with the first sunrays its *Ocean-tide*, of pikes, and fusils, *flows* glittering from the far east ;—immeasurable ; *born of the Night!* They march there, the grim host ; Saint Antoine on this side of the river ; Saint Marceau on that ; the black-browed Marseillese in the van. With hum, and grim murmur, far heard ; like the ocean tide, as we say ; drawn up *as if by Luna and Influences from the*

126

great Deep of Waters, they roll gleaming on ; no King Canute, or Louis, can bid them roll back. Wide - *eddying side - currents* of onlookers roll hither and thither, unarmed, not voiceless ; they, the *steel host*, roll on.

Grand old Carlyle. In spite of his German idiom he is the strongest, the most imaginative, the most virile, the most poetical prose writer the world has ever known.

As I have said, the figurative style appeals to the imagination. When we read that a horse's neck is clothed with thunder we get no definite idea, but only a general impression of force and rage and violence. The imagination clothes the animal with the attributes of furious war ; we see a horse who is something more than Bitzer's "quadruped," who is indeed the symbol and embodiment of equine strength and fierceness.

On the other hand, the literal style appeals to the memory. Whitman's gull "oscillating his body" is an example of close observation and of faithful and felicitous expression ; but its excellence can only be appreciated by one who has seen a gull, and has noticed its action in flight. We *see* without observing, or remember without knowledge, the spokes of light that play round the reflection of our heads in the water. It is only when Whitman reminds us of these things that our memory awakens and confirms his picture. But to a man who had never been on the water Whitman would appeal in vain. The fact is, language cannot convey to the mind a true conception of anything which the eye has not seen. That is why literal description depends upon the memory.

The power of language is very limited. It is very difficult to suggest sound, or convey an idea of colour or motion. There is no word to describe the flight of the swallow. To say that he wheels, or glides, or flies, or swims, or darts, or skims through the air, is ineffective. The pigeon wheels, the hawk darts, the gull swims, but none of these birds resemble the swallow in his flight.

Jefferies gives a very happy suggestion of

the lark's song when he speaks of his
"balancing himself on his trembling wings
outspread a few yards above earth, and
uttering that sweet little loving kiss, as it
were, of song." But Jefferies, artist as he
was, felt fully the poverty of language for his
purpose, and, in his article on " Nature and
Books," describes how he tried, and failed,
to give the colour of the common May
dandelion. He says—

Often, in writing about these things, I have felt
very earnestly my own incompetence to give the
least idea of their brilliancy and many-sided colours.
My gamut was so very limited in its terms, and
would not give a note to one in a thousand of those
I saw.

Then he tried books on colour, books on
optics, books on art, even painting pieces of
paper with colours—in vain, and goes on to
say—

Would it be possible to build up a fresh system of
colour language by means of natural objects ? Could
we say pinewood green, larch green, spruce green,
wasp yellow, humble-bee amber ? And there are

fungi that have marked tints, but the Latin names of these agarics are not pleasant. Butterfly blue—but there are several varieties; and this plan is interfered with by two things: first, that almost every single item of nature, however minute, has got a distinctly different colour, so that the dictionary of tints would be immense; and next, so very few would know the object itself, that the colour attached to it would have no meaning.

Again he says—

There are a million of books, and yet with all their aid I cannot tell you the colour of the May dandelion. There are three greens at this moment in my mind: that of the leaf of the flower-de-luce, that of the yellow iris leaf, and that of the bayonet-like leaf of the common flag. With admission to a million books, how am I to tell you the difference between these tints?

And any artist will tell us that in any one of these leaves there may be a dozen tints; the red glow of the sunset or vivid blue of the sky may be reflected, or there may be warm shadows of trees, or cool shadows of rocks, or the endless play and fluctuation of sunbeam, or water shine, so that to paint the surface of one broad dock-leaf we may have to go all round the palette.

As with colour, so with motion. We see writers employ the one word "rushing," to describe the motion of the express train, of a flight of swallows, and of a river in flood.

Rossetti said he hated long poems. I hate long descriptions. Life is too short to read reams of fine phrases about the Alps and the Rhone. Moreover, these tedious detailed descriptions fail of their purpose, for the mind cannot hold an extended word picture, and while the writer is putting in every fern leaf and foam sparkle of the cascade, the reader has entirely lost sight of the pinewood and the moor. Of course, if the writer's object is to display his own knowledge of nature and command of style, elaborate word pictures may serve his turn ; but if his object is to convey to the reader's mind a definite conception of a scene or a thing, it will pay him to be terse.

In descriptive writing the best plan is to seize upon the salient features of the object, and describe them in the fewest and aptest words the writer can command. The fewer the words the better. To swaddle an idea in a multitude of words destroys the effect, just as covering the fist with a boxing-glove deadens the blow. When you wish to make a strong, keen, and enduring impression upon the reader's mind, strike with the naked idea.

The earth was without form, and void, and darkness was upon the face of the deep.

You will find many such gems upon the stretched forefinger of Time, such as Shakespeare's figurative line (borrowed from Chaucer), which tells how the flowers

Do paint the meadows with delight ;

or that beautiful line of Cervantes'—

His face was like a benediction ;

or the Psalmist's

Battle upon a thousand hills ;

or Caryle's

Flesselles, pale to the very lips ;

or Erckmann and Chatrian's Prussian soldier, in the wood—

132

Taking aim at me, with a wrinkling of the eyes.

A writer should give the reader's imagination some scope, letting him fill in the picture for himself. Take these lines from Carlyle—

Wretchedness cowers into truckle-beds, or shivers hunger-stricken into its lair of straw.

Surely that rapid sketch is sufficient. No need to paint for us the bare garret or reeking cellar, no need to put in every bit of drawing; the lean, bony figure, the clinging rags, the fevered eyes glaring under their sombre porch of matted hair—you have it all there: the poverty, the misery, the hunger, the cold, the night, the darkness, the squalid lair, the furtive sidelong glance, the crouching form, the slinking action. To describe these things in detail, even tersely, as I have sketched them here, destroys the picture. Because thought is so much swifter than language, and so the imagination fills up an outline instantaneously, supplying shadow and colour with one flash, and keeping the impression,

133

whereas in plodding over words the vivid-ness of the effect is lost.

Down to the low lane, where, in her door-sill, the aged widow, knitting for a thin livelihood, sits to feel the afternoon sun,

says Carlyle again, and the picture is perfect, and brings at once to the imagination the bent form, the sunken features, the wrinkled hands, and clean, faded clothing of the poor old mother, warming her thin blood in the sunshine. Let us remember this nimble-ness of the imagination, and give it play. Gilbert White never overloads the theme with language. He says of the blue tit—

It will also pick holes in apples left on the ground, and be well entertained with the seeds on the head of a sunflower.

The blue tit perched on the sunflower is picturesque enough in its own simplicity of idea, and White does not spoil it. He does not add a word. In fact, the chief secret of good descriptive writing is knowing what to leave out. And that knowledge may be gained to some extent by study and practice. But a master is born as well as made, and no amount of study would enable any but a master to write such lines as—

Oh, ye divine ether, and swift-winged breezes,
And countless dimplings of the waves of the deep.

Mediocrity might study Prometheus for a leash of generations, but would never get the grand manner. Inspiration is not to be learned. A tortoise may pass a sleeping hare, but a crow can never sing the song of the skylark.

This matter of descriptive writing is one in which I have taken great interest, and to which I have devoted much study. My favourite masters are Gilbert White, Carlyle, Thackeray, and Erckmann and Chatrian. *The Conscript* and *Selborne* are veritable textbooks of the art. Add to them *Catherine*, *Sartor Resartus*, and some poetry, Shakespeare and Solomon first of all, then Milton and Spenser, and the student will need no further guides but practice, observation, and his own good sense and industry. But it is a difficult art, and one in which most of us can never be more than careful journeymen.

Gilbert White's descriptive work is mostly confined to the natural history subjects. It is often said that this descriptive writing, as applied to Nature, is comparatively modern. In *My Study Windows*, Lowell (Walter Scott, 1s. 6d.), there are some interesting remarks upon this subject from which I propose to quote—

The love of Nature in and for herself, or as a mirror for the moods of the mind, is a modern thing . . . The author of the Book of Job is the earliest I know of who showed any profound sense of the moral meaning of the outward world ; and I think none has approached him since, though Wordsworth comes nearest with the first two books of the "Prelude." . . . But the British poet Thomson ("sweet-souled," is Wordsworth's apt word) was the first to do with words what they (the painters) had done with colours. . . . He was the inventor of cheap amusement for the million, to be had of All-out-doors for the asking. It was his impulse which unconsciously gave direction to Rousseau, and it is to the school of Jean Jacques that we owe St. Pierre, Cowper, Châteaubriand, Wordsworth, Byron, Lamartine, George Sand, Ruskin—the great painters of ideal landscape.

136

I do not wholly agree with Lowell here. I think Thomson wrote landscape because the time was fit; and that Cowper, who was only thirty-one years behind him, would have done it had Thomson never been born. Just as Milton did it, and did it much better, a long century before Thomson drew his first breath. But at anyrate Gilbert White was born twenty years later than Thomson, and I don't think he owed his love of Nature or power of description to any he that ever wagged a chin. Indeed, Dan Chaucer, who, as Lowell himself says, was a fine scene painter, did his work three centuries before Thomson's time.

WHITE'S "SELBORNE"

THE "life" of Gilbert White resembles the "life" of Shakespeare in its mute eloquence. There is no matter for the biographer, *because* there is so much for the critic. The man's *real* life is his book. He put his whole soul into his work. The *Natural History of Selborne* is the record of his loves, his labours, and his days. All else that remains of him will make no more than the entries in a Registrar's Report.

Gilbert White was the eldest son of John White of Selborne, and of Anna, daughter of the Rev. Thomas Holt, rector of Streatham, in Surrey. He was born at Selborne on the 18th of July 1720; was educated at Basingstoke; went to Oriel College, Oxford, in 1739; was Bachelor of Arts in 1743, Fellow of his College in 1744,

Master of Arts in 1746, and a Senior Proctor of his University in 1752.

Three years later he became Curate of Faringdon, retaining the appointment for twenty-nine years. In 1784 he became Curate of Selborne. The last thirty-eight years of his life appear to have been passed in his native village. He died on the 26th of June 1793, in the seventy-third year of his age. He was never married, and his life and work are an exemplification of Bacon's rule as to those who "marry and endow the State."

A gentle, studious, unambitious man, he spent his days in the zealous and faithful study of Nature, for her own sake, and died leaving the precious results of his modest industry for the instruction and delight of posterity.

Why is Gilbert White a classic? Of his status as a scientific naturalist I know nothing. Personally, I have no scientific knowledge of natural history. Pure science has no charms for me. Darwin was a great man; but I cannot read his books. Nor can I believe that my favourite naturalist owes his niche in the temple of fame to science.

In the preface to the "Scott" edition of White's *Natural History of Selborne*, Richard Jefferies speaks to the value of White's labours as a naturalist thus—

A great master is under a disadvantage. You go to look at an old and celebrated picture with exalted feelings, and when you get there you say, "How disappointing! I have seen all this before." . . . The secret is, the old master's work has been multiplied exceedingly, and used as the groundwork on which to build innumerable variations. Without his work these could never have come into existence. From the stores accumulated by Gilbert White a very great deal of the contents of modern books have been drawn. Not only the facts, but the general system has been followed out in a hundred ways, so that his book suffers exactly like the old picture, until you understand it.

Jefferies also says—

If, on the other hand, your mind dwells upon science, and you feel yourself well-armed with argument, then you may find in Mr. White's books a number of facts which will give you plenty of occasion for exercising ingenuity. He will do more;

he will suggest to you the way in which to make original notes—the spirit in which to look at nature. Part of his success was owing to his coming to the field with a mind unoccupied. He was not full of evolution when he walked out, or variation, or devolution, or degeneration. He did not look for microbes everywhere. His mind was free and his eye open.

Doubtless Gilbert White was a great naturalist. Yet I do not think that fact has preserved his work still green in the affections of his countrymen after more than a hundred years. There have been many good naturalists whose works are not classics. Gilbert White owes his unique position to his amiable personality and his high literary excellence. The *Natural History of Selborne* appeals to the artist, to the lover of English, and to the lover of Nature. There are three special excellences in all his work—

1. The faculty of sweet and clear expression.

2. The faculty of picturesqueness.

3. The faculty of graphic and swift delineation.

His English is strong, pure, and musical. He possesses a happy choice of synonym, a wonderful aptness of words. His style is masterly in its clearness, terseness, and elegance. He conveys his ideas with a few firm and vivid strokes, selecting the salient points and picturesque features with unerring instinct, and using the right words always. Compare his work with Ruskin's. The latter burdens his subject with a bewildering magnificence of metaphor and fancy, graces and embellishes it with a gorgeous opulence of phrase, but his pictures, though more dazzling, are neither so vivid nor so informing as those of White. The difference between the two men seems to be that Ruskin possesses facility, and White felicity, of language. The latter seems to have striven not for elegance, or euphony of diction, but for precision of terms. His object was to make faithful studies, not ideal pictures. He combines scientific accuracy of observation with high artistic power of description and poetical sweetness of expression. His scrupulous care in the selection of

142

the *best* word is well exemplified in his letter
to Mr. Pennant on that author's new edition
of the *British Zoology—*

> When you say that in breeding-time the cock snipes
> make a bleating noise and a drumming (*perhaps I
> should have rather said a humming*), I suspect we
> mean the same thing.

Doubtless they did *mean* the same thing,
but White best described that thing.

Jefferies defends White's style. He says
of the note on the garden fauvet—

> Such is his way of putting a pretty little incident,
> and I want to point out that, as a matter of style,
> which is so much talked of nowadays, it is very
> much superior to the stiffest writing of the nineteenth
> century.

And of course it is superior to the "stiffest"
writing, but this will not content the admirers
of Gilbert White. It seems very cold praise.
White is a master of style, and in his own
line has no equal.

Lowell, who does not seem to have understood White at all, nor to have even suspected
his true excellence, says of the *Natural
History of Selborne—*

I used to read it without knowing the secret of the pleasure I found in it, but, as I grow older, I begin to detect some of the simple expedients of this natural magic. Open the book where you will, it takes you out of doors. In our broiling July weather one can walk out with this genially garrulous Fellow of Oriel, and find refreshment instead of fatigue. . . . I do not know if his descriptions of scenery are good, but they have made me familiar with his neighbourhood.

You will find the article I quote from in the "Scott" edition of *My Study Windows.* Mr. Lowell's patronage is irritating. He never grew old enough to discover the true "expedients" of that natural magic. He thoroughly exposes the falsity of his estimate of White when he calls him "garrulous." That is just the thing which White was not. He was sententious. Lowell himself is as garrulous as a cathedral guide. He chatters like a whole colony of rooks, and stuffs his articles with miscellaneous quotation and allusion, as if he had modelled his style upon the anatomy of melancholy. He was a clever and amusing writer, and a thoughtful and acute critic; but we cannot allow him to patronise his betters. White would say more, and teach more, in five lines than Lowell could in five pages.

I will now quote a few specimens of White's sweet and sound English—

The cart-way of the village divides, in a very remarkable manner, two very incongruous soils. To the south-west is a rank clay, that requires the labour of years to render it mellow ; while the gardens to the north-east, and small enclosures behind, consist of a warm, forward, crumbling mould, called black malm.

One can fairly see that black, rich earth, and feel it crumble through the fingers. But the marvel of these sentences is that such a subject as the difference betwixt two kinds of earth can be described at once so accurately and so sweetly, for the words read as musically as verse.

Here are some more earth notes, equally true, and equally pleasant to read ; notice the conciseness, the closeness with which our author packs his facts together, and the neatness and grace of the arrangement—

Still on to the north-east, and a step lower, is a kind of white land, neither chalk nor clay, neither fit for pasture nor for the plough, yet kindly for hops, which root deep into the freestone, and have their poles and wood for charcoal growing just at hand. This white soil produces the brightest hops.

As the parish inclines down towards Wolmer Forest, at the juncture of the clays and sand, the soil becomes a wet sandy loam, remarkable for timber, and in-famous for roads. . . . Beyond the sandy loam the soil becomes a hungry lean sand, till it mingles with the forest.

In his note on the old oak tree, in the Second Letter, the three excellences I have named are all combined—

In the centre of the village, and near the church, is a square piece of ground, surrounded by houses, and vulgarly called the Plestor. In the midst of this spot stood, in old times, a vast oak, with a short squat body, and huge horizontal arms, extending almost to the extremity of the area. This venerable tree, sur-rounded with stone steps, and seats above them, was the delight of old and young, and a place of much resort in summer evenings ; where the former sat in grave debate, while the latter frolicked and danced before them.

There is a simple picture, simply and truly drawn, in few and well-chosen words.

The black-cap has, in common, a full, sweet, deep, loud, and wild pipe ; yet that strain is of short continuance, and his motions are desultory; but when that bird sits calmly, and engages in song in earnest, he pours forth very sweet, but inward melody, and expresses great variety of soft and gentle modulations, superior, perhaps, to those of any of our warblers, the nightingale excepted.

That description is as sweet and wild as the song of the black-cap himself. A marvellous bit of writing; at once rhythmic, melodious, and unaffected in style, and complete in its entire realisation of purpose.

Here is a picture of some house-swallows, clustered on a willow branch—

His attention was first drawn by the twittering of these birds, which sat motionless in a row on the bough, with their heads all one way, and by their weight pressing down the twig, so that it nearly touched the water.

Here is another, that of the garden fauvet mentioned by Jefferies—

This bird much resembles the white-throat, but has a more white, or rather silvery breast and belly; is restless and active, like the willow wrens, and hops from bough to bough, examining every part for food. It also runs up the stems of the crown imperials, and putting its head into the bells of those flowers, sips the liquour which stands in the nectarium of each petal.

Here is a sketch of a titmouse—

The great titmouse, driven by stress of weather, much frequents houses; and in deep snows, I have seen this bird, while it hung with its back downwards (to my no small delight and admiration), draw straws lengthwise from out the eaves of thatched houses.

Of the swallow he writes—

Avenues and long walks, under hedges, and pasture fields, and mown meadows, where cattle graze, are her delight.

These pictures of White's remind one of what he himself says of the "sharp and stridulous" shrilling of the field-cricket; they "marvellously delight" the reader, "filling his mind with a train of summer ideas of everything that is rural, verdurous, and joyous."

Let us now seek a few examples of our author's masterly command of the art of graphic and swift delineation. His unrivalled power of producing vivid and true thumb-nail sketches from Nature.

At the same time let it be understood that the only purpose of this article is to intro-duce such of my readers as may not have met the Rev. Gilbert White, to the master himself. To appreciate the *Natural History of Selborne* at its true value, one must read it all; and read it again and again. No system of extracts, no eulogy or disquisition can bring one so near to a work as does the study of the work itself. To display a rose as earnest of a garden is well ; but the rose looks better on its stem, and gains as much from its back-ground of brown earth, or sombre foliage, or from its surroundings of stately lilies and humble moss, as the garden gains from its own sweetness and voluptuous loveliness.

White's book is as homely and as whole-some as fresh cream and brown bread and butter, as luscious and as dainty as a dish of strawberries, or a bunch of meadow-sweet or corn-flower.

Of course one must bring some taste, as well as appetite, to the feast. A madrigal is nothing but a noise to the man that hath no music in his soul. *Selborne* is a dull and bald catalogue to him that has neither artistic feeling nor imagination. The great charm of the book, indeed, as I hinted before, lies in the fact that the author trusts the reader, leaving something to his imagination.

Perhaps the best comparison I can make is that used by me in a previous article—the comparison of White's method of description to the Japanese method of painting. Take a picture of a stork or a bullfinch as painted by an English artist. It is more accurate, more detailed than a painting of the same bird by a Japanese. But in the matter of the representation of life the Japanese excels our men a hundredfold. Even our flying birds are painted as if they hung upon wires. They are models, and models of stuffed birds. The birds of the Japanese painter are somewhat crude in drawing and broad in treatment, but they are alive, their throats are flexible, their plumage is downy, their breasts seem to palpitate, their eyes to sparkle, and when they are painted flying one can almost hear the rustling of their wings.

The cause of this difference is simple.
The English artist studies and paints birds
chiefly from dead models. The Japanese
goes to the aviary and watches hour after
hour and day after day until he masters
the secrets of bird life ; the air, the motion,
the balance and *feeling* of the creatures.

So it was with Gilbert White. He did
not see Nature through another's eyes, nor
get his natural history from books. He
went to the fields, and to the woods, and
went again, and yet again, setting down only
what he *saw*. Let me quote again from the
preface to his book by Richard Jefferies—

Mr. White took much interest in swallows. Not
only one evening, or two evenings, but a whole year
of evenings, and several years, are written in these
letters. So quiet, without excitement—he is ready to
wait till next year, or a series of years, to verify anything he supposed might be ; something so entirely
opposed to the modern lecturer. He gathered his
facts very slowly ; they were like experience, which
takes a lifetime to grow. You cannot sit down and
make up experience, and write it as a thesis ; it must
come ; and this is what he did—he waited till things
came. His book, for this reason, reads as if it had
been compiled in the evening.

This is high praise, but it is true. Gilbert White never seems to have counted the cost of time and labour. He never thought about his own fame, about his own talent, about his own devotion. He loved Nature with all his heart, and gave all his days to her service, calmly, patiently, and cheerfully, and who shall say that he did not well?

I am glad Jefferies chose the swallow letters for his eulogy of our author's method. Jefferies himself wrote some magnificent chapters on swallows. His description of the swallow's flight is a marvel of keen insight and close study. I have read nothing finer on that fascinating subject; and yet—

And yet; those swallows! No one has described them; no one has sung their praises worthily. That fatal poverty of language. It makes us impotent. What can we say of our feelings towards the ocean, the swallow, or the rose? How can we pluck out the heart of Nature's mysteries, and cage her wild force and heavenly beauty in mere twigs and wires of words.

The swallow is a wonder and a delight to

me. I could watch these ineffably swift,
beautiful, and graceful creatures on the wing
for hour after hour. They fill me always
with a vague yearning, a strangely mingled
feeling of loving admiration and unquench-
able desire. If I could but fly with them
for one sunny hour ! If I could but understand their language ! Times out of number
have I stood and watched them dipping and
flashing and gliding and wheeling in the sunshine and sweet air, and wondered, and
wondered, *what* do they mean ? What are
they ? Why am I doomed to crawl like a
caterpillar on this dull clay ball, and envy
these children of the air their joy, and
speed, and power of flight ? Think of it.
The glory of the sudden turn, the swift
rise, the wide circle in the warm, spicy air,
and then the long, long dive, fifty feet down
from the crown of the elm to the nodding
plumes of the scented clover ! No, we
know nothing of the swallow. He baffles
us, delights us, tantalises us with his
superiority ; and then when the grey web
of the winter begins to weave in the corner

of the sky, he shakes his glossy wings and swims away in the golden track of departing summer.

But this is not my business. I return to the study of dear old Gilbert White. *He* never fretted, nor envied, nor complained. He was like brave old Whitman, and his life speaks out to us the sentiment of the American master's mighty lines—

> The earth, that is sufficient for me,
> I do not want the constellations any nearer.

He admires and loves the wild things and fair flowers of the earth, but always calmly, cheerfully, and without excitement. A patient, wise, and placid man—

I was much entertained, last summer, with a tame bat, which would take flies out of a person's hand. If you gave it anything to eat, it brought its wings round before the mouth, hovering and hiding its head, in the manner of birds of prey when they feed.

The grasshopper lark began his sibilous note in my fields last Saturday. Nothing can be more amusing than the whisper of this little bird, which seems to be close by, though at a hundred yards' distance; and when close at your ear is scarcely any louder than when a great way off. Had I not been a little ac-

quainted with insects, and known that the grasshopper kind is not yet hatched, I should have hardly
believed but that it had been a *locusta* whispering in
the bushes. The country people laugh when you tell
them that it is the note of a bird. It is a most artful
creature, skulking in the thickest part of a bush, and
will sing at a yard distance, provided it be concealed.
I was obliged to get a person to go on the other side
of the hedge where it haunted ; and then it would run,
creeping like a mouse before us for a hundred yards
together, through the bottom of the thorns ; yet it
would not come into fair sight ; but in a morning
early and when undisturbed, *it sings on the top of a
twig, gaping, and shivering with its wings.*

Of the two willow-wrens known to him,
White says—

No two birds can differ more in their notes, and
that constantly . . . for the one has *a joyous, easy,
laughing note*, the other *a harsh, loud chirp.*

That shows swiftness of description and
felicity of language indeed. So of the reed
sparrow ; we are told that he

Has *a variety of hurrying notes*, and sings all night.

Here is a suggestive little picture of the
departing swallows—

155

At the dawn of day, which was foggy, they rose altogether in infinite numbers, occasioning such a rushing, from the strokes of their wings against the hazy air, as might be heard to a considerable distance.

Here another, of a different kind—

The white owl does indeed snore and hiss in a tremendous manner ; and these menaces will answer the intention of intimidating, for I have known a whole village up in arms on such an occasion, imagining the churchyard to be full of goblins and spectres.

I regret, with Jefferies, that White did not also write a natural history of the *people* of Selborne. It would have been invaluable.

The voice of the goose is trumpet-like, and clanking.

A perfect suggestion of the sound. But here, now, is a bit of painting in our author's best manner—

The evening proceedings and manœuvres of the rooks are curious and amusing in the autumn. Just before dusk they return in long strings from the foraging of the day, and rendezvous by thousands over Selborne Down, where they wheel round in the air, and sport and dive in a playful manner, all the while exerting their voices and making a loud cawing, which, being blended and softened by the distance that we at the village are below them, becomes a confused noise or chiding, or rather a pleasing murmur, very engaging to the imagination, and not unlike the cry of a pack of hounds in hollow, echoing woods, or the rushing of the wind in tall trees, or the tumbling of the tide upon a pebbly shore.

For felicity and purity of language, for simple and limpid flow of sentences, for close and faithful description of the subject, for aptness and beauty of similitude, and for the wonderful concentration of the sounds and sights of country life within a narrow compass, that passage seems to me to be unrivalled. It is a masterpiece, and so typical of the many excellences of Gilbert White's writings, that further citation is superfluous.

Lowell, in his article on Thoreau, says of the American writer—

He had caught his English at its living source, among the poets and prose-writers of its best days; . . . his metaphors and images are always fresh from the soil; he had watched Nature like a detective who is to go upon the stand; as we read him, it seems as if all out-of-doors had kept a diary and become its own Montaigne; we look at the landscape *as in a Claude Lorraine glass ; compared with his all other books of similar aim, even White's " Selborne," seem as dry as a country clergyman's meteorological journal in an old almanac.*

As I remarked above, Lowell was a good critic, and a clever writer; but he was an American, and doubtless it is because Thoreau paints American scenery, and White English scenery, that Lowell finds the former so much more interesting than the latter.

Thoreau is one of my favourites, and his work is good; but we cannot allow such an injustice as this sacrifice of the master to the apprentice. That Thoreau studied White seems probable; that he improved upon him, no admirer of *Selborne* will allow.

The two men were essentially different. Each loved Nature in his own way; but White was satisfied with loving service, Thoreau seems to have expected wages in the shape of public applause. Our man honoured his goddess with priestly worship; the American seems rather to have exhibited her as a showman. White described a thing either to inform the reader or to glorify

Nature; Thoreau seems to have desired as much admiration for his own art as for the beauty of his subject. White was a born artist, but did not know it. He sat down to make loving and faithful studies as a naturalist, and produced pictures because he could not help being picturesque. Thoreau was a born and *practised* artist, and made his pictures deliberately, with an eye to colour and composition. The pictures in *Walden*, though beautiful, are neither so frank nor so pure as those in *Selborne*, because White thinks *only* of his work, while Thoreau thinks chiefly of *himself*. Thoreau takes his easel into the woods to paint exhibition pictures; White goes out with a sketch book to do " illustrations." He says, a white-throat is like *this*, and draws it exquisitely. If he puts it on a thorn-branch, it is because he finds it there; and he never puts anything into a drawing but what he *sees*.

In *Baker Farm* Thoreau says—

Sometimes I rambled to pine groves, standing like temples, or like fleets at sea, full rigged, with wavy

boughs, and rippling with light, so soft and green and
shady, that the Druids would have forsaken their oaks
to worship in them; or to the cedar wood beyond
Flint's pond, where the trees, covered with hoary
blue-berries, spiring higher and higher, are fit to stand
before Valhalla, and the creeping juniper covers the
ground with wreaths full of fruit; or to swamps
where the usnea lichen hangs in festoons from the
white spruce trees, and toad-stools, round tables of
the swamp gods, cover the ground.

Compare that elaborate picture with the
graphic and simple work of Gilbert White.
Our man was content with the trees and the
birds. He would not have dragged in the
Druids, nor the swamp gods, nor Valhalla.

Thoreau's pictures of the wild woods and
their wilder denizens are very fine, but he
constantly spoils the canvas by putting in his
own figure. It has the same effect as the
sudden appearance of the operator's thumb
across the lens of a magic lantern. One
grows weary of his introspection. One
resents his thrusting of his puny, greedy,
eager soul, betwixt one's gaze and Nature.

The wildest scenes had become unaccountably
familiar. I found in myself, and still find, an instinct

towards a higher, or, as it is named, spiritual life, as do most men, and another towards a primitive rank and savage one, and I reverence them both.

Thoreau's philosophy is very well, his thought is strong and clear, his independence very healthy and robust ; but who wants to be preached at about the strivings of the soul, when the noble trees are waiting to be seen and loved ?

In my opinion Thoreau is best when he is most like Gilbert White.

A little flock of these titmice came daily to pick a dinner out of my wood-pile, or the crumbs at my door, with faint, flitting, lisping notes, like the tinkling of icicles in the grass.

That is perfect, and in White's own manner ; so, also, in his note on the hovering of the phœbe—

Sustaining herself on humming wings with clinched talons, as if she held by the air.

But it has not White's *freshness*.

In the account of the merlin's flight we seem to get a blend of White and Ruskin—

L   161

It was the most ethereal flight I had ever witnessed. It did not simply flutter, like a butterfly, nor soar like the larger hawks, but it sported with proud reliance on the fields of air ; mounting again and again with its strange chuckle, it repeated its free and beautiful fall, turning over and over like a kite, and then recovering from its lofty tumbling, as if it had never set its foot on *terra firma*. It appeared to have no companion in the universe, sporting there alone, and to need none but the morning and the ether with which it played. It was not lonely, but made all the earth lonely beneath it. Where was the parent which hatched it, its kindred, and its father, in the heavens ? The tenant of the air, it seemed related to the earth, but by an egg hatched sometime in the crevice of a crag ; or was its native nest made in the angle of a cloud, woven of the rainbow's trimmings and the sunset sky, and lighted with some soft midsummer haze caught up from earth ? Its eyrie now some cliffy cloud.

Which again is very fine—writing. But it *is* writing, with an artful employment of alliteration and cadence, of which our good old Gilbert was as innocent as a meadow lamb is of the wiles of a Covent Garden dancer.

No, we cannot put this piping bullfinch, piping the tunes he has learned, above our

English skylark of Selborne, who sings his wild and sweet songs because his soul is made of melody and his world is fair. *Selborne* is a classic; the more ambitious *Walden* is not. White is a *master*; Thoreau is only an artist. Thoreau's powers can be taught, such genius as Gilbert White's is born.

There; I have tried my best to give you good reasons why the *Natural History of Selborne* is one of my favourite books. As for criticism, I have none to offer. Gilbert White will do for me just as he is. He never wrote a line I should wish to see changed, or could expect to see improved.

SIR THOMAS BROWNE

THERE is an edition, in one volume, at 1s. 6d., of Sir Thomas Browne's *Religio Medici*, *Urn Burial*, *Dreams*, and *Christian Morals*, which is published by Walter Scott in his Scott Library, and may be ordered from the *Clarion* Office, by post 1s. 8d.

Sir Thomas Browne was a scholar and physician. He was born in London on the 19th October 1605, and died at Norwich on the 19th October 1682. As a writer he was contemporary with Milton, Jeremy Taylor, Selden, and Fuller.

Living in and through the stormy times of the Civil War, Sir Thomas appears to have held aloof from politics.

Lowell says of Gilbert White, who calmly ignored the American War of Independence, that he took more interest in "the natural

164

duration of a hog's life" than in the struggle of his own brothers for the possession of a continent; and in the same spirit did Sir Thomas Browne, with the din of battle often in his ears and all England ablaze with religious and political fanaticism, sit tranquilly in his study at home, writing such thoughts as might come to a lonely anchorite in some mountain solitude, far from the bubbling caldron of life, and nearer to the stars of heaven than to the Star Chamber of King Charles. One wonders what kind of uproar or peril could have driven this calm philosopher from his studies. Perhaps he too, like Madam Roland, would have paused at the scaffold's foot to ask for pen and paper with which to record his thoughts.

It is as a prose stylist that Sir Thomas Browne is most distinguished. His style is one of our literary landmarks. His prose is of Milton's kin, sonorous, exuberant, splendid; and comes just after Sidney, Raleigh, and Bacon, and just before Bunyan. His work, like a beautiful half-way house, gilded gorgeously, graced with fantastic carvings, and sumptuously coloured, stands between the wild, luxuriant loveliness of Elizabeth's literary architects and the ordered grace and sober elegance of Dryden's building.

I am to give the reasons of my love for this author's book. The value of every author consists in his thought or his expression; in what he says, or how he says it, or both.

Sir Thomas Browne's tone of thought is one of serene gravity, relieved and lighted by flashes of quaint and often humorous fancy. He gives old truths a new meaning, shows us familiar things in strange lights, startles us with novel and unexpected views of things long known. His earnestness has a fine quality of dignified restraint, his wisdom is spontaneous, unobtrusive. His smile is frequent, but quiet and half hidden; it flickers in soft sparkles from the deeps of his thought, like the glint of a trout's gold armour far down in the river shadows under the solemn trees. Sir Thomas has irony, Sir Thomas has wit; but Sir Thomas is always

an artist, always a scholar, always a perfect
gentleman. "All haste is vulgar," says
Ruskin, and might have added, "all noise."
Sir Thomas Browne is never vulgar. He is
never noisy, and he is never in a hurry.

The salient characteristics of Sir Thomas
Browne's style are picturesqueness and
melody.

Melody is the quality of musical prose,
and arises from the cunning manipulation
of verbal sounds, and the mastery of
rhythmical pause and cadence.

Picturesqueness is the faculty of suggest-
ing pictures to the mind by the use of metaphors, similes, and allusions.

The secret of prose melody is known to
few, but the effect is apparent to all who
have good ears. In all melodious passages
we shall find skilful repetitions, skilful variations, and skilful alternations of verbal
sounds. Vowel sounds are of two kinds:
light and heavy, grave and gay; the deft
handling of these sounds is almost an art in
itself. Variation of the heavy vowels aids
melody, alternation of light and heavy

vowels aids melody, alternation of vowels and liquids aids melody. Repetition and alliteration aid melody.

The broad vowel sounds may be heard in the following words: arm, aim, eel, all, own, ooze, oil, owl, isle, tune.

The short vowels may be heard in gnat, net, knit, knot, nut, foot.

As a rule the short vowels accelerate, and the long vowels retard, the movement of the sentence. Their use has, therefore, much influence on the cadence and pauses of prose.

Vowels are sometimes varied to give tune, and sometimes repeated to give alliteration in a passage. I will give examples of both uses. Here is an example of variation of vowel sounds: "As the dry grass sinks down into the flame and is consumed."

Here the vowel sounds run: I, Ah, Ow, A, U.

Here is an example of repetition of the vowel sounds: "Or ever the silver cord be loosed, or the *golden bowl* be *broken*." Here the sound of the three o's in "golden bowl be broken," not only gives tune by alliteration, but also suggests the deep clang and chime of stricken metal.

Alliteration means the repetition of like sounds or letters. Repetition means the repeating of identical sounds, or words, or phrases. Examples of repetition are common in the best prose. As, "Set me *as a seal* upon thine heart, *as a seal* upon thine arm."

Again, "*And the* almond tree shall flourish, *and the* grasshopper shall be a burden, *and* desire shall fail"—

Again, "Or ever the silver cord *be loosed, or the* golden bowl *be broken, or the* pitcher *be broken* at the fountain, *or the* wheel *broken* at the cistern."

In this last example we have repetitions of the phrases "or the" and "be broken." The word "be" occurs three times, "or" four times, "broken" three times, and there are two "at's" and six "the's"; yet it is one of the most musical and perfect prose passages ever written.

Alliteration is of several kinds. There is initial alliteration, which is repetition of an initial letter, as in " Labour low levels loftiest longest lines."

There is secondary alliteration, as in "At last we all in still tranquillity shall sleep."

In the first of these examples we have the easiest and commonest form of alliteration, the sounds running: lab, low, lev, lof, long, line.

In the second example the alliteration is concealed, the sounds running: la, all, ill, il, all, slee.

But alliteration has forms more subtle still. Take, for instance, Pope's line—

The harsh, rough verse should like a torrent roar.

In this line we have seven r's, yet only two of them are initials.

Let us now take a passage of Sir Thomas Browne's and examine it. Speaking of some bones discovered in a tomb, he says they have outworn strong and spacious buildings, "and quietly rested under the drums and tramplings of three conquests."

This is melody. Let us see if we can find

whence the melody arises. Nearly all words holding the sound of "q" are melodious, as "quaint," "quarrel," "antiquity," "sequestered." And in this line we find "quietly" and "conquest." Then we have four alliterative r's in res, rum, ram, and ree; we have the humming "m" in drums echoed sharply in tramplings; we have "rest" and "quest," and we have a pattering series of short vowels suspended and pointed by the long "e" in "three."

So much for the melody. Sir Thomas's art makes the line sing like a tune. Now for the quality of picturesqueness.

Sir Thomas might have said "and have rested peacefully for a thousand years," or, "and have rested quietly for ages during which the land they lay in was thrice conquered." But he is an artist in pictures as well as in sounds, and he suggests the dead men sleeping quietly in the silence of the grave *under* "the drums and tramplings of three conquests." So the quiet is broken to our ear by the drums and tramplings, and we see the mail-clad horsemen whirling, struggling, and stabbing, the dip and swoop of the banners, the sunlight flashing on spear and crest, and our ears are filled with the roll of drums and clash of steel, and our minds take in the large idea of long duration, of deeds and destinies sweeping over the earth like turbulent seas, while at the same time we feel the presence only a few feet under the sod of those stark, still figures, blind and dumb, sleeping "quietly," in a kind of sad ironic silence. How much more expressive is the phrase "three conquests" than any statement of time in bald figures; and the thought of the dead sleeping quietly under the drums and tramplings, what contrast it gives, what meaning it carries, what suggestion and picture in a few sweet words.

As I said the other day, books like these cannot be written hurriedly, nor for pay. Sir Thomas Browne wrote quietly in his own study at home, for his own pleasure, and the amusement of a few friends, and with no idea of publication. He wrote at his ease, and for the love of writing, and his whole literary output is not equal in volume to one year's work of a modern author. There were no journalists in those days, and no log-rollers, and men made books as they make cloaks and swords and oaken cabinets—*to last.*

Coleridge, himself a consummate artist, as well as a profound and acute critic, has left in some marginal notes written in a copy of *Religio Medici* a very just and sympathetic estimate of Sir Thomas Browne. He first complains that Sir Thomas is *hyperlatinistic.* This is true. As Johnson said, Browne used a quantity of " exotic words," and, continued the doctor, "his style is indeed a tissue of many languages, a mixture of heterogeneous words, brought together from distant regions, with terms originally appropriated to one art, and drawn by violence into the service of another."

This charge is quite just. It is true also, and a droll fact it is, that Dr. Johnson himself was enamoured of Latin words, that he founded this style upon that of Sir Thomas Browne, and that in the matter of pedantry he was little better, and in the

173

pomp and circumstance of glorious verbiage much worse than his master.

I may pause here to offer a few remarks upon the qualities of the two great English styles in literature—the severely Teutonic, or Saxon, and the profusely exotic or Latin. In the Saxon short words predominate, in the Latin polysyllables are numerous. For ordinary use the Saxon style is better, but in special cases, and in the hands of genius, the Latinised English yields magnificent effects. Bunyan and Defoe we would not alter; but we love our Browne and Milton in their gorgeous foreign embroideries, and would not for a great deal allow the sacrilegious hand of the commentator to blot a line of *Areopagitica* or *Urn Burial*.

Sir Thomas Browne, like Carlyle, Ruskin, and Dickens, is dangerous to imitate, but he is beautiful to read; and he is best to read in the night when the house is still and the melodious sentences may sing in the ear and cloy the mouth with sweetness, and when the quick succession of quaint and lovely fancies may march through the mind, rank

174

behind rank, to the chime and rhythm of the enchanted verbal music, like the triumphal harmonic sequence of some glorious organ fugue.

To return to Coleridge. I quote the following snatches from his "note" :—

> He is a quiet and sublime *enthusiast*, with a strong tinge of the *fantast*—the humorist constantly mingling with, and flashing across, the philosopher, as the darting colours in shot silk play upon the main dye . . . reading nature neither by sun, moon, nor candlelight, but by the light of the faëry glory around his own head, so that you might say that nature had granted to *him*, in perpetuity, a patent and monopoly for all his thoughts.

Coleridge concludes his note with a quotation from the "Quincunxes," which affords a fine example of the quaintness—or, as Coleridge expressed it, "*the Sir-Thomas-Browneness*"—of our author's best passages. Here is the finale of the "Quincunxes," as quoted by Coleridge—

> But the quincunx of heaven (*the Hyades, or "five stars," a constellation just above the horizon at midnight*) runs low, and 'tis time we close the five parts

175

of knowledge. We are unwilling to spin out our waking thought into the phantasms of sleep, which often continueth precogitations, making cables of cobwebs, and wildernesses of handsome groves. To keep our eyes open longer were to act our antipodes! The huntsmen are up in America, and they are already past their first sleep in Persia.

Of this curious and beautiful passage Coleridge says—

Was ever such a reason given before for going to bed at midnight? To wit, that if we did not we should be acting the part of our antipodes! And then, "*the huntsmen are up in America*"—what life, what fancy. Does the whimsical knight give us thus the *essence* of gunpowder tea, and call it an *opiate*?

Now, note the quaintness, the delicate subtlety of that short passage; note also the aptness of the language, the strange kind of moonlight, fairy mist of an atmosphere the thoughts make for themselves. Sir Thomas, sitting silent in his study at midnight, seems half to think and half to croon his fancy of the strange distortions which a dream makes of a waking thought—"making cables of cobwebs, and wildernesses of handsome groves"—"To keep our eyes open longer."

—Sir Thomas is not nodding; he is thinking
in a waking dream—"To keep our eyes open
longer were to act our antipodes."—The
mischievous knight has his eyes half shut.
The long Greek hiss of antipodes breathes
out in a languorous sigh, like the sound of
thin, spent waves on sand, and then—
suddenly, without warning, leaping from the
drowsy dream shadow, as Falstaff's knaves in
Kendal Green leapt from the gloom of nowhere—with startling unexpectedness come
the words: *"the huntsmen are up in
America!"* It is magic. Gone the dim
study, the brooding author, the eerie moon-
shine; and behold the dawnshine on the
copper pillars of the pine woods, the horizon
aflame with amber light, the zenith a sea of
quivering blue fire, and the keen-eyed, swift-
footed red-skin, gun in hand, parting the
long grasses and hallooing his mustang to
the chase. "And they are already past their
first sleep in Persia." Oh, rare Sir Thomas.
So, after all, we finish with heavy hangings,
mossy carpets, a scent of roses, a silken
couch, and a drowsy snore.

M　　177

The element of surprise is one of Sir Thomas Browne's favourite devices. You never can guess what he is going to say next. In his thought it is the unexpected which commonly happens. His range, too, is almost limitless. He will go to the ends of the universe or the horizon of time for a simile or an illustration. To grace his sentence or point his thought, he will fly to the North Star, dive to the bottom of the Pacific, or snatch a hair from the Great Cham's beard. He has a marvellous eye for colour, a marvellous hand for pictures, and is past-master of "the well-enchanting skill of music." His memory is like a museum of odd facts and quaint imaginings, the scope of his conception is as wide as the heavens, and in his best passages his fancy flames and sparkles, and changes form and colour like a catharine wheel, or we might say that he juggles with queer metaphors, and foreign words, and learned allusions, and cunning cadences with the skilful ease and certain grace of an Eastern juggler playing with knives and balls. His rhythm has the regu-

178

lar irregularity of the rolling seas; his wit and fancy resemble the phosphorescent lights which illuminate and glorify the waves.

Here are some examples of his quality. To match the whimsical humour of the passage quoted by Coleridge, take the following :—

Even such [*of the dead*] as hope to rise again, would not be content with central interment, or so desperately to place their relics as to lie beyond discovery and in no way to be seen again ; which happy contrivance hath made communication with our forefathers, *and left unto our view some parts which they never beheld themselves.*

No head but Sir Thomas Browne's could have bred the idea of our seeing the bones of our fathers which our fathers never saw, nor could any pen save his so quaintly have expressed it. Again—

The Scythians, who swore by wind and sword, that is, by life and death, were so far from burning their bodies that they declined all interment, and made their graves in the air ; and the Ichthyophagi, or fish-eating nations about Egypt, affected the sea for their grave, thereby declining visible corruption, and *restoring the debt of their bodies.*

179

That last conceit would have pleased Hamlet.   So would the following :—

To burn the bones of the King of Edom for lime seems no irrational ferity; but to drink of the ashes of dead relations a passionate prodigality.   (*As Artemesia of her husband Mausolus.*)

In the following the author's simile seems rather rueful, perhaps involuntary :—

To be gnawed out of our graves, to have our skulls made drinking bowls, and our bones turned into pipes, to delight and sport our enemies, are tragical abominations escaped in burning burials.

That is hardly what one looks for in a treatise on cremation; but how picturesque it is, how virile.   And here is a " Sir-Thomas-Browneish " means of expressing time—

And Charles the Fifth can never hope to live *within two Methuselahs of Hector.*

The following grave reflection, read at night, and abed, always makes me laugh :—

In vain do individuals hope for immortality, or any patent from oblivion, in preservations below the moon; men have been deceived even in their flatteries, above the sun, and studied conceits to perpetuate their names in heaven. The various cosmography of that part hath already varied the names of contrived constellations; Nimrod is lost in Orion, and Osyris in the Dog-Star. While we look for incorruption in the heavens, we find they are but like the earth—durable in their main bodies, alterable in their parts, whereof, besides comets and new stars, perspectives begin to tell tales, and the spots that wander about the sun, with Phaeton's favour would make clear conviction.

But let us seek some sublimer passages. With what lurid imagination is the following sentence lighted :—

When many that feared to die shall groan that they can die but once, the dismal state is the second and living death, when life puts despair on the damned; when men shall wish the coverings of mountains, not of monuments, and annihilations shall be courted.

"When life puts despair on the damned . . . and annihilations shall be courted." Sir Thomas paints his hell with epic fire upon a background of impenetrable and hopeless shadow. Hell was a reality to men in his day.

But Sir Thomas was not always dreamy and imaginative. He could think also, and strongly, as the following quotations prove :—

From *Urn Burial*.

Who knows whether the best of men be known, or whether there be not more remarkable persons forgot than any that stand remembered in the known account of time? Without the favour of the everlasting register the first man had been as unknown as the last, and Methuselah's long life had been his only chronicle.

From *Christian Morals*.

Value the judicious, and let not mere acquests in minor parts of learning gain thy pre-existimation. 'Tis an unjust way of compute to magnify a weak head for some Latin abilities, and to under-value a solid judgment because he knows not the genealogy of Hector. When that notable King of France would have his son to know but one sentence in Latin ; had it been a good one, perhaps it had been enough. Natural parts and good judgments rule the world. States are not governed by ergotisms. Many have ruled well who could not, perhaps, define a commonwealth ; and they who understand not the globe of the earth command a great part of it. Where natural logic prevails not, artificial too often faileth. When nature fills the sails, the vessel goes smoothly on ; and when judgment is the pilot, the insurance need not be high.

Where industry builds upon nature, we may expect pyramids; where that foundation is wanting, the structure must be low. They do most by books who could do much without them; and he that chiefly owes himself unto himself is the substantial man.

Christian Morals.

Affection should not be too sharp-eyed, and love is not to be made by magnifying glasses. If things were seen as they truly are, the beauties of bodies would be much abridged. And therefore the wise contriver hath drawn the pictures and outsides of things softly and amiably unto the natural edge of our eyes, not leaving them able to discover those un-comely asperities which make oyster shells in good faces and hedgehogs even in Venus' moles.

If our wise knight's wisdom like you, try his eloquence. The following flawless jewels of style are earnest of the wealth any reader may with a little patience dig from the mine beneath the covers of this wondrous volume :—

Now, since these dead bones have already outlasted the living ones of Methuselah, and, in a yard under ground and thin walls of clay, outworn all the strong and spacious buildings above it, and quietly rested under the drums and tramplings of three conquests, what prince can promise such diuturnity unto his relics, or might not gladly say—

" Sic ego componi versus in ossa velim ? "

Time, which antiquates antiquities, and hath an art to make dust of all things, hath yet spared these minor monuments. . . . If they fell by long and aged decay, yet, wrapped up in the bundle of time, they fall into indistinction, and make but one blot with infants.—*Urn Burial.*

We whose generations are ordained in this setting part of time are providentially taken off from such imaginations ; and being necessitated to eye the re-maining part of futurity, are naturally constituted unto thoughts of the next world, and cannot ex-cusably decline the consideration of that duration, *which maketh pyramids pillars of snow, and all that's past a moment.—Urn Burial.*

The italics are mine. The words "con-sideration" and "duration" ought not to come so near together. They destroy the euphony ; but the end of the sentence is fine thought, picturesque imagination, and pure melody.

But man is a noble animal, splendid in ashes, and pompous in the grave, solemnising nativities and deaths with equal lustre, nor omitting ceremonies of bravery in the infamy of his nature.—*Urn Burial.*

184

There is a noble sentence. It is like the thought of Solomon set to Chopin's music.

That children dream not the first half-year; that men dream not in some countries, with many more, are, unto me, sick men's dreams; *dreams out of the ivory gate, and visions before midnight.—On Dreams.*

The close of that sentence is like a verse from the Song of Songs. It has the beauty, the dignity, the mournful cadence of "Though a man should give all the substance of his house for love, it would utterly be contemned."

The finest example of sustained eloquence in Sir Thomas Browne's book is the peroration (Chap. V.) to *Urn Burial.* As a display of picturesque and melodious style it would be difficult to match. It is one magnificent blaze of literary fireworks, and cannot be appreciated except as a harmonious and consistent whole. It must be read again and again—and always in quietude, when the house is still and the mind is free of petty worries and the fear of interruption. I will quote two passages here — but, remember,

they belong to a large design, and they may
not be relished nor assimilated in a noisy
workshop, nor amid the oscillation and rattle
of a train—

What song the Syrens sang, or what name Achilles
assumed when he hid himself among women, though
puzzling questions, are not beyond all conjecture.
What time the persons of these ossuaries entered the
famous nations of the dead, and slept with princes
and councillors, might admit a wide solution. But
who were the proprietaries of these bones, or what
bodies these ashes made up, were a question above
antiquarism; not to be resolved by man, nor easily,
perhaps, by spirits, except we consult the provincial
guardians, or tutelary observators. Had they made
as good provision for their names as they have done
for their relics, they had not so grossly erred in the
art of perpetuation. But to subsist in bones, and be
put pyramidally extant, is a fallacy in duration. Vain
ashes which in the oblivion of names, persons, times,
and sexes have found unto themselves a fruitless con-
tinuation, and only arise unto late posterity as emblems
of mortal vanities, antidotes against pride, vainglory,
and madding vices. . . .
Circles and right lines limit and close all bodies,
and the mortal right-lined circle (*the sign or figure of
death*) must conclude and shut up all. There is no
antidote against the opium of time, which temporally

186

considereth all things. Our fathers find their graves
in our short memories, and sadly tell us how we may
be buried in our survivors. Gravestones tell truth
scarcely forty years. Generations pass while some
trees stand, and old families last not three oaks. To
be read by bare inscriptions like many in Gruter, to
hope for eternity by enigmatical epithets, or first
letters of our names, to be studied by antiquaries,
who we were, and have new names given us, like
many of the mummies, are cold consolations unto the
students of perpetuity, even by everlasting language.

To be content that times to come should only know
there was such a man, not caring whether they knew
more of him, was a frigid ambition in Cardan, dis-
paraging his horoscopal inclination and judgment of
himself. Who cares to subsist like Hippocrates'
patients, or Achilles' horses in Homer, under naked
nominations, without deserts and noble acts, which
are the balsam of our memories, the *entelechia* and
soul of our subsistence? To be nameless in worthy
deeds exceeds an infamous history. The Canaanitish
woman lives more happily without a name than
Herodias with one. And who had not rather have
been the good thief than Pilate?

But the iniquity of oblivion blindly scattereth her
poppy and deals with the memory of men without
distinction to merit of perpetuity. Who can but pity
the founder of the pyramids? Herostratus lives that
burnt the Temple of Diana; he is almost lost that
built it. Time hath spared the epitaph of Adrian's

187

horse, confounded that of himself. In vain we compute our felicities by the advantage of our good names, since bad have equal durations, and Thersites is like to live as long as Agamemnon.

With such serene wisdom and jewelled eloquence Sir Thomas wrought amid the "drums and tramplings" of the Civil War. Rupert, with dare-devil bravery, led victorious charges, "returning to find his camp in the possession of the enemy." Charles the First intrigued and lied, commanded, fled, and went to prison and the block. Cromwell sprang from obscurity into the fierce light of fame; beat down with mailed fist the divinity that doth hedge a king; dragged England, as though by the hair of her head, with stripes and exhortations, to the premier place in Europe; saw his heroes of the bilboe and the Bible "drive before them in headlong rout the finest infantry in Spain"; refused the crown and took the kingship; died, and sought his narrow bed of clay. Charles the Second came to his own, and played ducks and drakes therewith. Milton hurled pamphlets like javelins at his enemies, and wrought immortal poems in his blindness. Hampden fought and died, the Ironsides triumphed and were disbanded, and all the while the wise knight, Sir Thomas Browne, sat snug and unruffled in his study, writing musical *hic jacets* over the "pride, vainglory, and madding vices" of poor humanity. "There was something sad about the hour, and something strange about the man."

Mr. Walter Pater, in his thoughtful essay (*Appreciations*: McMillan & Co.), alludes to Browne's golden phrasing as "unpremeditated wild flowers of speech." But they are more than that; they are unpremeditated wild flowers of thought and speech. It is the thought that is so poetical, so strangely individual, so picturesque. But the words in which the thought is presented are so felicitous, so consonant with the meaning, so melodious, that word and phrase appear inseparable. Indeed, in Sir Thomas's "wild flowers of speech," the word befits the meaning as the perfume of the brier rose befits its beauty. Note the following from *Christian Morals* :—

189

There is but one who died salvifically for us, and able to say unto death, "Hitherto shalt thou go, and no farther"; only one enlivening death, which makes gardens of groves, and that which was sowed in corruption to arise and flourish in glory—when death itself shall die and living shall have no period; when the damned shall mourn at the funeral of death; when life, not death, shall be the wages of sin; when the second death shall prove a miserable life, and destruction shall be courted.

Sir Thomas Browne has been frequently compared to Montaigne. The two men are alike in their candour, their sincerity, their artless confidence in the reader; but Sir Thomas, to me, seems more akin to Gilbert White, and it may be said of *Urn Burial,* as of the *Natural History of Selborne,* that ostensibly written as a scientific treatise on a given question, it has become a classic by reason of its unique artistic excellence and literary charm.

THE "PILGRIM'S PROGRESS"

I FEAR I cannot approach the *Pilgrim's Progress* with the same critical calm with which I approached *Urn Burial*. I was turned of forty year, and somewhat of a writer and student myself, when Sir Thomas Browne was introduced to me, but Bunyan was the friend and teacher of my childhood; the *Pilgrim's Progress* was my first book. It was for me one of the books to be "chewed and digested," and in my tenth year I knew it almost all by heart.

In the house where I lodged at that time there was a baby, and because its mother was necessarily much from home, and I was an obliging boy, with little business and much mischief on my hands, I often, very often, found myself acting as nurse to this unknown and nameless child.

191

Whether the child was boy or girl I cannot remember, neither can I recall its mother's name or condition; but I know I used to sit by the hour to rock its cradle, and that I used to study the *Pilgrim's Progress* as I rocked.

More than that, growing fond of the helpless, inarticulate little bundle of pink pulpiness, as I should in a short while have come to love a dog, or a doll, or a broken knife, I used at times, when the baby was restless, to ride it upon my knee, and recite to it passages out of Bunyan, or sing to it the verses—they are but feeble poetry—from that wonderful book, to tunes of my own composing.

Every word that Bunyan wrote he believed, every incident of his great allegory was real to him. And it was all as real and true to me. Armed with two feet of broken stage sword-blade, and wearing a paper helmet and breastplate, I went out as Greatheart and did deeds of valour and puissance upon an obsolete performing poodle, retired from Astley's Circus, who was good enough to double the parts of Giant Grim and two lions.

The stairway to the bedroom was the Hill Difficulty, the dark lobby was the Valley of the Shadow, and often I swam in great fear and peril, and with profuse sputterings, across the black River of Death which lay between kitchen and scullery.

The baby also, poor, unconscious mite, played many parts. Now it was Christiana, and had to be defended against the poodle at the point of the sword; now it was Faithful being tried for his life; now it was Ignorance crossing the Black River in a cradle boat rowed by myself as Vain-Hope; and anon it was Prudence and Charity buckling on my harness before I went out to fight and vanquish Carlo (as Apollyon) in the Vale of Humiliation. If that baby didn't dream dreams it must have had no more conceit in it than a mallet.

Well, all things considered, I cannot be expected to review the *Pilgrim's Progress* as I should review a new novel by Beatrice Harraden or Thomas Hardie. Criticism of

N 193

Bunyan's work is beyond me. I might as well try to criticise the Lord's Prayer, or "The House that Jack Built," or "Annie Laurie."

As I bethink me, however, I am not asked to criticise, but to expound. Very well. To thoroughly appreciate the *Pilgrim's Progress* one should first of all know something of the life and character of John Bunyan, and of the times he wrought in. To this end I should advise the student to read a good modern biography of our author, also his own *Grace Abounding*, and, this essentially, the sympathetic and informing review of Southey's edition of the *Pilgrim's Progress* in the *Essays* of Lord Macaulay.

The *Pilgrim's Progress* itself can be got at a low price. The Chandos edition, Warne & Co., published at 2s., is a very good one.

John Bunyan was born at Elstow, in Bedfordshire, in 1628. He died in London in 1688. His parents were very poor people. They taught him to read and write, and that comprised his education. He seems to have been a wild, but not a wicked boy; but his conscience was so quick and his imagination so strong that he magnified the venial offences of an uncouth village lad into deadly sins. In his youth he served as a soldier in Cromwell's army, and was present at several engagements; after that he was a travelling tinker, until being converted by the Baptists he became a powerful and most eloquent preacher.

In the year 1660 he was arrested for preaching, and was sent to Bedford Jail. Here he was shut up for twelve years, and here he wrote the *Pilgrim's Progress.* It is probable that the book was written in the first years of his captivity, but it was not published until 1678, six years after his release, and then its publication was opposed by Bunyan's friends, whose Puritan ideas were averse to it as being in some sort a romance, and therefore sinful.

Bunyan lived in a time of fierce religious intolerance and political strife. During his sixty years of life Charles I. was dethroned and beheaded; Cromwell was made Protector, died, was dug up and hanged at

Tyburn; Charles II. was banished and restored, and died; James II. came to the throne, and was ousted by William of Orange.

Bunyan saw the Parliamentary War, and served in it; lived through the wars of Cromwell in Ireland and Scotland, the wars against Spain and Holland, the Covenanters' Rebellion, the Rye House Plot, the Monmouth Rebellion, and the "Bloody Assize" of the infamous Lord Jeffrys; and died while the "Glorious Revolution" was in progress.

He was contemporary with Cromwell, Milton, Sir Thomas Browne, Hobbes, George Herbert, Sir Isaac Newton, Evelyn and Pepys, Defoe, Dryden, Hampden, Blake, Waller, Jeremy Taylor, Herrick, George Fox, the first Quaker, Izaak Walton, Fuller, Addison, Congreve and Wycherly, Samuel Butler, Judge Jeffrys, and Locke.

While he was in prison Charles II. was restored, Cromwell's body was exhumed, the Great Plague ravaged England, the Great Fire nearly destroyed London, the Dutch fleet entered the Medway, Van Tromp and De Ruyter "smoking victorious pipes as far up an English river as Sheerness," Addison was born, Milton published *Paradise Lost*, and the first plays of Congreve and Wycherly were produced.

The period is that described in *The Three Musketeers* and *Lorna Doone*.

It was a period of battles, plots, intrigues, barbarities, and persecutions, and it may well be said of the tinker - parson, John Bunyan, "happy his grace that could translate the stubbornness of fortune into so quiet and so sweet a style."

The subjoined table of events may be useful to the busy reader :—

1628. Bunyan born.
1628. Cromwell M.P. for Huntingdon.
1631. John Dryden born.
1633. G. Herbert's poems published.
1633. G. Herbert died.
1641. John Evelyn began his diary.
1642. Sir Isaac Newton born.
1643. Sir T. Browne's *Religio Medici* published.
1643. Chalgrave Field, death of Hampden.
1644. Battle of Marston Moor.

197

1644. Milton's *Areopagitica* published.
1645. Bunyan a soldier.
1645. Battle of Naseby.
1645. Edmund Waller's poems published.
1647. Jeremy Taylor preaching.
1648. Herrick's *Hesperides* published.
1648. Lord Herbert of Cherburg died.
1649. Charles I. beheaded.
1649. Cromwell in Ireland.
1650. Bunyan joins the Baptists.
1651. Battle of Dunbar.   Cromwell in Scotland.
1651. Hobbes' *Leviathan* published.
1652. War with the Dutch.   Blake defeats Van Tromp.
1652. George Fox founded the Quakers.
1653. Bunyan becomes a Baptist minister.
1653. Three days' battle with Dutch in the Channel. Blake defeats Van Tromp.
1653. Izaak Walton's *Compleat Angler* published.
1655. Cromwell's soldiers rout the Spanish.
1657. Cromwell, Lord Protector.
1658. Sir Thomas Browne's *Urn Burial* published.
1658. Death of Cromwell.
1660. Bunyan sent to prison.
1660. Dryden began to write.
1660. Charles II. restored.
1661. Cromwell's body hanged at Tyburn.
1661. Daniel Defoe born.
1662. Fuller's *Worthies* published.

1665. Outbreak of the Plague.
1666. The Great Fire of London.
1666. The Dutch in the Medway.
1667. Milton published *Paradise Lost.*
1672. Bunyan is released from Bedford Jail.
1672. Addison born.
1672. George Fox goes to America.
1672. Congreve and Wycherly's plays begin.
1674. Butler's *Hudibras* published.
1674. Death of Milton.
1678. "Pilgrim's Progress" published.
1679. Covenanters' Rebellion.
1679. Samuel Pepys imprisoned.
1680. Samuel Butler died.
1683. The Rye House Plot.
1685. Titus Oates tried.
1685. Monmouth Rebellion.
1685. Jeffrys goes the "bloody assize."
1685. Charles II. died.
1685. James II. crowned.
1685. Louis XIV. of France revoked the Edict of Nantes, thus depriving Protestants of the little liberty they possessed.
1687. Edmund Waller died.
1687. Publication of Sir I. Newton's *Principia,* proving law of gravitation.
1688. Bunyan died.
1688. William of Orange landed.
1690. Locke's *Essay on the Understanding* published.

Bunyan was a man of abnormal imagination. His imagination was vivid, active, flaming, Dantean. It gave light,—often lurid light,—and heat, and form, and colour to all he saw. It made his thoughts stand out in blazing, sun-bright relief, or sink into seas of gloomy shadow ; it gave glory, and sweetness, and celestial tone to all his joys, and it put cruel edge and piercing point on all his sorrows. He was a nervous man, too ; one whose soul-harp was high-strung, answerable in quivers of pain, and shrieking sharps of repulsion to every jar or discord; and his conscience was a lynx-eyed tyrant, unsleeping and remorseless. An enthusiast, struggling with bared head and sensitive hands through a storm of tyrannies ; an excitable nature in a feverish time, there is small wonder if John Bunyan painted in lamp - black and lightning, in blood and tears. Swords and psalms, self - accusations, fervid prayers, unmeasured' invective, cruel revenges, iron-fisted persecutions were the commonplaces of his youth's environment ; and with little education, and fitful counsel, he moved,

200

dreaming in a fearful wakefulness, through scenes of battles, plots, assassinations, unjust trials, brutal executions, jails, sins, conversions, and fiery preachings. Under different conditions, in a calmer age, he would have done marvels, but we should never have had a *Pilgrim's Progress.* It was the surroundings of his life, the character of his contemporaries, the uproar and agitation of his times that made him what he was and his book what it is.

It was because of his low birth, his scanty culture, his impressionable and imaginative nature, his life of warfare, persecution, and imprisonment, and because of the dread shadow of the gloomy and fearful Calvinistic faith which fell across his path, that his own pilgrimage was one of sins magnified through mists of terror, of self-tortures, despondency, doubts, backslidings, of trials, of perils, and frantic wrestlings with the devil and his own spirit, of valiant endurance and stubborn endeavour, and of final victory and peace in faith. And just what his own pilgrimage had been his book became. Christian is

201

Bunyan, and Christian's progress is a vivid and imaginative portrayal of the travail and the tribulations, the failures and the triumphs, the dragon-slaying and poison-drinking, the fiend - resisting and God - forsaking, and the humblings and repentances which were the bitter and the sweet experiences of his own strenuous and eager soul.

What are the chief literary characteristics of John Bunyan's book? Sincerity and imagination. That which he wrote he believed. Had he not lived it? Into what slough of despond he fell in his youth; how he lost heart and went back to his worldly habit of life; what he endured in Doubting Castle, is all written in his *Grace Abounding*, as plainly as in the allegorical *Pilgrim's Progress*. And as to this latter book, was he not in an Ogre's den when he wrote it; consigned thereto, after a shameless mockery of a trial, by some Hate-Good of an intolerant fanatic? That Bunyan was in earnest in his history of that strange life's - pilgrimage of Christian is natural enough if we remember that he was recounting those mishaps and adventures which befell himself. Neither must we forget that times are changed with us. Bunyan had reason for his hostility to Popery; and all the dangers and terrors of a Christian's road in his day were actual and apparent. As I have said, he was in jail for conscience' sake when he wrote, and every day Faithfuls were being done to death in Vanity Fair.

But apart from personal causes, Bunyan's literary method was distinguished by a naïve sincerity. Note the description of the side door of hell which the shepherds show to Christian: "They looked in and saw that within it was very dark and smoky; they also thought that they heard there a rumbling noise as of fire, and that they smelt the smell of brimstone." And note again the account of the colloquy by the silver mine, and of Giant Despair's courtyard "paved with the skulls of murdered pilgrims." Bunyan tells all his wonders with a childlike good faith, never doubting he will gain belief. He tells them simply, as men tell facts; not ornately or cunningly, as artists write stories.

There is not in the *Pilgrim's Progress* a single speck of the garish colours of romance. To its author the story was not a romance. It was a true story, his own story, told allegorically, but without the smallest attempt at conscious embellishment. Such art or device as the work contains was the direct result of the author's own innate genius. He was a born story-teller, with an imagination so virile and magnificent as to impose upon his own judgment.

There is a similar reason for the belief accorded to the *Pilgrim's Progress* by readers of all classes, creeds, and races.

Which of us has not soiled his garments in the Slough of Despond? Which of us has not, as Christian did, taken hands to help his feet up the steep sides of Hill Difficulty? Which of us has not turned from the little wicket in hopes to sneak round by a flowery and level way? Which of us has not drowsed in the enchanted ground; listened to blasphemies of the devil, and thought them our own sin; quaked and held the sword-hilt sternly in the Valley of the Shadow; fallen, clutching sand and bruising our bones in the Valley of Humiliation; wrestled with Apollyon, and suffered falls and wounds? Which of us has not funked the chained lions, dared the devils of the pit, squandered money and time upon the gew-gaws and follies of Vanity Fair, fallen into the clutches and under the cudgel of Despair, and rested for a brief while upon the Delectable Mountains, looking out wistfully for the distant glamour of the Golden Gate?

What is the experience of Teuffelsdröch in *Sartor Resartus* but the experience of Christian spoken in another tongue? Read in *The Everlasting No—*

Thus has the bewildered wandered to stand, as so many have done, shouting question after question into the Sibyl-cave of Destiny, and receive no answer but an echo. It is all a grim desert, this once fair world of his; wherein is heard only the howling of wild beasts, or the shrieks of despairing, hate-filled men; and no pillar of cloud by day, and no pillar of fire by night, any longer guides the pilgrim.

This is Christian in Doubting Castle. Turn to *The Everlasting Yea,* and we find

Christian again; but now he is free, and walks sword on thigh to do his duty and to win his way—

Here, then, as I lay in that CENTRE OF INDIFFER-ENCE, cast, doubtless by benignant Upper Influence, into a healing sleep, the heavy dreams rolled gradually away, and I awoke to a new Heaven, and a new Earth.

The first preliminary moral act, Annihilation of self, had been happily accomplished, and my mind's eyes were now unsealed, and its hands ungyved.

It is the old good fight of faith; it is the perennial, untiring, ever-green story of a human soul's temptation, suffering, and endeavour. It is what all children love, "A story about themselves."

In the characters of Bunyan there are the same truths and sincerity, the same naïve faith in the presentment of familiar types. His heroes are so *human*. They are always stumbling, erring, wavering, and falling into scrapes. Faithful is much taken with the plausible talk of Shame; Hopeful is vainglorious over the three thieves who rob Little Faith; and Christian! into what troubles does he blunder, and with what fickleness and tenacity, heroic cowardice, and intermittent constancy does he pursue his dangerous and trying journey. He falls and fails continually, and is always so sorry and so humbly frank of confession. The lions scare him, the leaning hill scares him; he goes into bypaths, and is taken prisoner; he gives way to despair, and counsels suicide in Doubting Castle; he follows the black man in the white raiment, and is snared in a net, but he perseveres very manfully. He fights Apollyon with sterling courage, and, though his faith and his valour are both almost drowned out of him in the black River of Death, he finally struggles through like a *man.*

It is because he is a man, and not a hero, a creature strong and frail, timid and brave, that we like him. Just in the same way do men love Robin Hood and King Arthur— for their failures and their faults as well as for their virtues, from sympathy with them in defeat as much as from admiration of them when victorious. Christian is a true son of

Adam—and of Eve. A poor, faulty, good brother of ours compounded all of earth and fire.

Of the minor characters not one is forced or artificial. Mr. Pliable we all know; he still votes for the old Parties. Mr. Worldly Wiseman writes books and articles against Socialism. Mr. Facing-both-ways is never absent from the House, and I think Mr. By-ends is become the guiding spirit of the British Press. Hear him—

It is true we somewhat differ in religion from those of the stricter sort, yet but in two small points: first, we never strive against wind and tide; second, we are always most zealous when religion goes in his silver slippers; we love much to walk with him in the street if the sun shines and the people applaud him.

The street he named must have been Fleet Street. But, again—

The worst that ever I did to give them an occasion to give me this name was that I had always the luck to jump in my judgment with the present way of the times, whatever it was, and my chance was to get thereby.

A Jubilee knight evidently, or a butterscotch peer. One can hear him saying, as By-ends says—

I shall never desert my old principles, since they are harmless and profitable.

"Harmless and profitable!" There is the philosophy of modern journalism in a nutshell. Let us be harmless; let us jump with the times; don't let us offend the advertiser; do let us walk with Religion when the people applaud him and the sun shines! This policy is profitable. It is also easy, and harmless.

But I think my special pet is Mr. Talkative, the man who says—

What you will. I will talk of things heavenly, or things earthly; things moral, or things evangelical; things sacred, or things profane; things past, or things to come; things more essential, or things circumstantial; *provided that all be done for our profit.*

The italics are mine. That little bit of cant is lovely. It is the one touch of humbug which makes the whole world kin. I have met that man. I have met him on platforms. I have heard him prate, and prate, and prate; and I have seen him posture and pose; and I have known all the while that this pitiful exhibition of vanity actually *believed* that he was "doing it all for our profit." He has done a great deal in his day, has Mr. Talkative, for the profit of Hansard.

In point of imagination Bunyan excels all the writers of his age, Milton alone excepted. Note his picture of the Valley of the Shadow of Death, with its gins, snares, and pitfalls; its lurid hell mouth; its hobgoblins and satyrs of the pit; its narrow path betwixt the quagmire and the ditch; its companies of fiends, heard, but not seen, approaching; its gloom, its smoke, its terror, and its "doleful noises and rushings to and fro." Note also his fight with Apollyon, and how the demon spreads his dragon's wings and flies away. Even the names of his places and his characters are vividly imaginative: "Vanity Fair," "The Delectable Mountains," "The Slough of Despond," "The Valley of the Shadow,"

"Giant Despair," are names that have stamped themselves upon the national memory.

But besides this wonderful faculty of imagination, Bunyan had another essential faculty of a good writer : the faculty of *selection.* Macaulay appears to have confused these two faculties. Speaking of the *Pilgrim's Progress,* he says—

> This is the highest miracle of genius, that things which are not should be as though they were, that the imaginations of one mind should become the personal recollections of another. And this miracle the tinker wrought.

Macaulay goes on to say that every place in the journey is real to us. This is true. We do know "every declivity, resting-place, and turnstile," as well as "the sights in our own street." Take, for instance, the stile over which Christian and Hopeful go into the territories of Giant Despair, and the footpath along by the hedge. Those things are as familiar to us as ways into the woods, or across the meadows, where we went as children to gather flowers.

How is this? What is the secret of such magic?

Macaulay appears to have put it down to imagination. The explanation is not so simple. What Macaulay calls the miracle wrought by the tinker was wrought by three faculties: imagination, sincerity, and artistic selection.

To convey the impression of reality to a reader's mind, to make the imaginary seem actual, to be what we now call "graphic," a writer must be an impressionist.

The secret of the "highest miracle of genius" lies in the capacity to seize upon the essentials of a picture, and present them vividly. The fewer the details the better; the fewer the words in which they are clothed the better. This is what the French critic meant when he said that literary genius consisted in knowing what to leave out.

In my article on White's *Selborne* I dealt with this subject, and contrasted the methods of White and Ruskin.

When White describes a landscape, or a

scene, we see it, and remember it. When Ruskin describes a scene we remember the beautiful language, but we have a dim conception of the object so copiously described.

He who would be graphic must be selective and brief.

The great essential is to acquire mastery in the use of detail. We remember many of Bunyan's scenes because he tells us so little about them. Of the Hill Difficulty he tells us nothing but that it was a hill and steep; of the footpath across the Giant Despair's demesne he tells us little but that it ran hard by a hedge; and we remember these things because we have all seen steep hills and hedgerow paths, and because we at once adopt a hill or a path from the pictures in our memories. It is small wonder, then, that these places are real to us. They *are* places we know, but they are *our* places, not Bunyan's, and real as they are to me, and real as they are to others, they are not the *same* to any two of us. Macaulay's Valley of Humiliation, Doubting Castle, and Hell Gate are not mine nor yours. Each of us paints his own picture, puts it into Bunyan's frame, and cries out " wonderful."

Don't imagine, though, that nothing is needed but a bald outline. Bunyan adds to the reality of his scene by the action of his characters. In the case of the stile and the footpath he impresses the scene upon us by making the pilgrims debate at the stile as to whether or not to cross it and leave the beaten way, and he makes them see that the path runs parallel to the road, and he puts a man on the path walking ahead of them, and he makes Hopeful differ with Christian about the way, and finally he brings the darkness down upon them. So that actually we remember the path by what occurred upon it, and we put in our own path for the actors to perform on.

I never read *any* description of the Dargai Heights, but I can *see* them ; and I can see the Garden of Maiwand. It is not the *real* garden, of course, nor is it the garden *you* can see ; but it will serve.

Here let me give one short extract from the work of a great master of detail. I mean Daniel Defoe. It is from the *Journal of the Plague Year*, and describes how Defoe went to a churchyard at night to see the dead buried. The sexton dissuades him, but he remains, and this is what he sees. And remember this is imaginary, for Defoe was a baby at the time of the Plague—

. . . I stood wavering for a good while ; but just at that interval I saw two links come over from the Minories, and heard the bellman, and then appeared a dead-cart, as they call it, coming over the streets—

Cannot you see those lights? Cannot you hear that bell? Cannot you see that dead-cart coming over from the Minories? Yes; and what is more, you can see the darkness, which is not mentioned, and the gables and chimneys of the houses, which are not mentioned, and you will remember the picture for years. Why?

Let us examine the picture. It is given in a few words, and there are but few details. But we find that not only is there no detail that does not tell in the effect, but that some

215

of the details suggest parts of the picture which the artist does not describe.

Thus the bellman suggests the awful tolling of the bell ; the two links suggest the darkness ; the mention of the Minories gives an air of truth to the sketch; and the dead-cart suggests the unnamed horror of its load.

Observe, also, the art of the sequence. First come two links, then the bellman, then the dead-cart, then the streets. The picture is complete, and one can only realise how good by discovering how easily it may be spoilt.

"Write it up" in the modern style, and see what the effect will be. Let me try what kind of a mess I can make of it :—

But at that moment I saw two torches come flickering out of the darkness, and heard the dismal tolling of the bell ; and directly afterwards from the black shadows of the street there appeared a dead-cart, its wheels jolting heavily on the broken way, and its driver slouching despondently by the side of the tired horses.

You see, I have carefully put in all that Defoe so carefully left out, and the result is

216

that the picture is commonplace ; it has lost its stern and striking contrasts of light and shade ; it is too definite, and it does not awaken the imagination, nor will it print itself upon the memory.

Study that short passage from Defoe. It is worth it. See how few the strokes of the brush. Two lights, a bell, a cart, a street, laid in in simple words upon a background of *suggestion.*

Bunyan gets his effects in a different way. He makes light and shade by alternating pleasant and unpleasant places. Thus the Leaning Hill and the Slough of Despond are followed by the Interpreter's House ; the Hill Difficulty by the House Beautiful ; the Green Valley of Humiliation by the Gloomy Valley of the Shadow ; the Sunny Land of Beulah by the cold, black River of Death. Yet Bunyan also could paint in miniature, as witness the Garden of Lilies : "On either side of the river was a meadow, curiously beautified with lilies, and it was green all the year long." There is no detail, no apparent art, but what a lovely little picture it is.

217

The characteristics of Bunyan's style are clearness, directness, and virility; but other qualities are present, and not seldom we come upon veins and sparkles of true poetic gold, as when we are told that "the clouds were racked and heaven in a burning flame."

Macaulay says—

The style of Bunyan is delightful to every reader, and invaluable as a study to every person who wishes to obtain a wide command over the English language. The vocabulary is the vocabulary of the common people. . . . Yet no writer has said more exactly what he meant to say. For magnificence, for pathos, for vehement exhortation, for subtle disquisition, for every purpose of the poet, the orator, and the divine, this homely dialect, the dialect of plain working men, was perfectly sufficient . . . no book which shows so well how rich our language is in its own proper wealth, and how little it has been improved by all that it has borrowed.

It is true that the homeliest English is good enough for every purpose of the poet, the orator, and the divine; and nothing but ignorance or idleness can account for the use of our modern newspaper jargon, and technical slang in works intended for the instruction of uneducated people.

There is hardly a book on economics, or on any subject of importance to working men, which would not be the better for careful translation into the English of Bunyan or of Defoe.

Sir Thomas Browne's sonorous and melodious sentences are a source of delight to scholars and to authors; but when a book is intended to appeal to the man in the street, it should be wrought out in hard - bitten, clean - cut Saxon English.

Socialist writers and speakers cannot too thoroughly learn this lesson.

Bunyan's English is tinker's, and soldier's, and preacher's English. It is the English of the Bible, of the Ironsides, and of the village green.

"A pitiful sneaking business," that is market, or tavern talk; "He would make my way bitter to my soul," that is Bible talk; but when Faithful answers his ac-

219

cusers he answers in the language of the Cromwellian troopers—

I say that the prince of this town, with all the rabblement, his attendants, are more fit for a being in hell, than in this town and country: and so the Lord have mercy upon me.

And there is an echo of Marston Moor in Apollyon's threat to Christian: "Here will I spill thy soul."

I cannot conclude this hasty review of Bunyan's book without comparing the style of the tinker with that of the scholar and poet, Milton.

I will quote first from Milton's prose masterpiece, the *Areopagitica*—

Methinks I see in my mind a noble and puissant nation rousing herself like a strong man after sleep, and shaking her invincible locks. Methinks I see her as an eagle mewing her mighty youth, and kindling her undazzled eyes at the full midday beam, purging and unscaling her long-abused sight at the fountain itself of heavenly radiance, while the whole noise of timorous and flocking birds, with those also that love the twilight, flutter about, amazed at what she means, and in their envious gabble would prognosticate a fear of sects and schisms.

220

Contrast that copious and splendid diction with the clear, simple strength of the following speech of Evangelist from the *Pilgrim's Progress* :—

My sons, you have heard, in the words of the truth of the Gospel, that you must, through many tribulations, enter into the Kingdom of Heaven. And, again, that in every city bonds and afflictions bide you ; and therefore you cannot expect that you should go long on your pilgrimage without them, in some sort or another. You have found something of the truth of these testimonies upon you already, and more will immediately follow ; for now, as you see, you are almost out of this wilderness, and therefore you will soon come into a town that you will by and by see before you ; and in that town you will be hardly beset with enemies, who will strain hard but they will kill you ; and be you sure that one or both of you must seal the testimony which you hold with blood ; but be you faithful unto death, and the King will give you a crown of life.

The English of Milton is more musical, more sumptuous, more stately ; but that of Bunyan is more direct and simple, and more likely to be "understanded of the people." Therefore, all who write for the people shall do well to study Bunyan.

221

ON REALISM

MR. MORRISON, the author of *A Child of the Jago*, has, it appears, been ticketed by the critics as a Realist. Sometimes, as he says, "in praise . . . and sometimes as a reproach never to be lived down." As realism cannot be at once creditable and discreditable to an author, Mr. Morrison is quite justified in asking his critics to explain what they mean when they call him a Realist.

What is a Realist? At first thought one would reply that a Realist is an author who portrays things as they really are. But how *are* they? No landscape is exactly the same thing to any two artists. No idea, character, act, consequence, scene, or moral produces exactly the same impression upon any two authors. Suppose, then, a place or person

222

to be described by a dozen novelists, from as many different points of view, with as many different results, who is to decide which of the twelve is the faithful witness —the Realist?

No; our first definition will not serve, and we must be content to define the Realist as one who describes things as they actually appear to *him.* Such a Realist is a literary witness who tells the truth, the whole truth, and nothing but the truth. Such faithful testimony is supposed in the case of an author when the term Realist is applied to him as a compliment.

As to what is meant by those who use the same word as a term of reproach, we cannot be so sure. But I think that an author is often reproached as a Realist when he indulges in a superfluity of detail, or when he describes sordid or repulsive facts plainly, or when he sacrifices the spirit of his subject to a slavish and laboured delineation of externals — as if a painter should offer an accurate anatomical study of a corpse as a picture of a living athlete.

With the spurious realism we need have
no concern at present. As for the true
realism, there is no such thing in English
literature, and I hope there never will be.
For the true realism, according to our
definition, must tell not only the real
truth, but the *whole* truth, of the matter
treated. Which brings me back to Mr.
Morrison. Mr. Morrison, after declaring
that he has never called himself a Realist,
writes thus—

I have been asked in print, if I think that there
is no phase of life which the artist may not touch.
Most certainly I think this; more, I know it. It
is the artist's privilege to seek his material where
he thinks well, and it is no man's privilege to say
him nay. If the community have left horrible places
and horrible lives before his eyes, then the fault is
that of the community; and to picture these places
and these lives becomes not merely his privilege,
but his duty. It was my fate to encounter a place
in Shoreditch, where children were born and reared
in circumstances that gave those children no reasonable chance of living decent lives; where they were
born foredamned to a criminal or semi - criminal
career. It was my experience to learn the ways
of this place, to know its inhabitants, to talk with

them, eat, drink, and work with them. For the existence of this place and for the evils it engendered the community was responsible, and every member of the community was, and is, responsible in his degree. If I had been a rich man I might have attempted to discharge my peculiar responsibility in one way; if I had been a statesman I might have tried another. Being neither of these things, but a simple writer of fiction, I endeavoured to do my duty by writing a tale wherein I hoped to bring the condition of this place within the comprehension of others. There are those who say I should have turned away my eyes and passed by on the other side, on the very respectable precedent of the priest and the Levite in the parable.

An infinite deal of nothing has been written about *A Child of the Jago.* The book has been foolishly praised, and as foolishly condemned, and both praise and condemnation have been a source of amusement and surprise to the few who possess real knowledge of both literature and the slums. For it is a fact within the memories of a legion readers that nearly every feature of the "Jago" life has been painted in literature before; and it is a fact within the knowledge of innumerable citizens of London,

Glasgow, Dublin, Liverpool, and Manchester, that the life of the "Jago," and of all other slums of which the "Jago" is a type, is more horrible, more miserable, more shameful, and more unspeakable than Mr. Morrison has painted it. Mr. Morrison's practice in the *Child of the Jago* is better than his theory in the above quotation, for he has *not* presented the "Jago" in all the colours of its wretchedness and shame. On the contrary, he has exercised a stern artistic reticence. He has been more reticent, by far, than I should be if I wrote of a similar district, and he has proved to the hilt my contention that complete and true realism in fiction is unbearable.

Let anyone who knows the slums consider how the truth is toned down or evaded in *A Child of the Jago*. What are the two commonest adjectives of the low-life Cockney? No publisher dare print them: yet in "Jago" conversation hardly a sentence is spoken without their use. And do women like Sally Green and Nora Walsh fight in silence, like bulldogs? I have known many

226

such, and I have heard them, under stress
of rage and gin, use language which I should
not like to repeat even privately and to one
of my own sex. Then nothing is said in
Mr. Morrison's book as to the sanitary
arrangements of the "Jago," nor is there
any indication of the great prevalence of
sickness, which is one of the commonest
characteristics of all slums. Sore eyes, sore
heads, scrofula, diphtheria, fever, rheumatism,
consumption, bronchitis, king's evil, and
other terrible and loathsome complaints
flourish in the slums as fungi flourish upon
rotten trees. In one district of Ancoats a
few years ago the lady visitors reported
sixty per cent. of the population as sick.
Finally, as to the "Jago" morals. Are the
smugs and the respectables of horrible
London shocked by the revelations as to
coshing and the laxity of the marriage tie?
But it is all true, and worse things are true
than any Mr. Morrison has told. For it is
true that in the "Jago" children are
prostitutes before they reach their teens;
and it is true that bad as are the morals of

227

the East, they are exceeded by the vileness of the West of London.

There is not a newspaper nor a novelist in these islands who dare tell the whole truth and the real truth about Whitechapel, the Strand, and Piccadilly. Are we to understand that the respectable old ladies of both sexes who in reviews have called *A Child of the Jago* improper and exaggerated, really know no more of London and of London life than they have made apparent in their articles? If so, where have the poor dears been hiding their innocent heads? And are their maternal parents aware of their absence from home?

If we turn from the censure of Mr. Morrison's book to the praise of it, we shall find equal reason for astonishment and protest. One critic sapiently observed that in discovering the "Jago" Mr. Morrison has proved himself a true literary explorer, and had discovered in our very midst an unknown country. In the *Revue des Deux Mondes,* M. T. de Wyzewa hails Mr. Morrison as the founder of " a new school of Realism." The

228

Scotsman, in its review of *A Child of the Jago*, says, "Since Daniel Defoe, no such consummate master of realistic fiction has arisen among us as Mr. Arthur Morrison," and as if this were not enough, adds, "There is all Defoe's fidelity of realistic detail, suffused with the light of a genius higher and purer than Defoe's."

Now, I cannot see that Mr. Morrison has discovered any new country, nor that he has founded any new school, nor that he is the most consummate master of realistic fiction since Defoe, nor that he has a higher and purer genius than the man who wrote *Robinson Crusoe* and *A Journal of the Plague Year*, and I propose to dispute these assertions, and, if possible, to disprove them.

First of all, a few words about Defoe. Why is Defoe always cited as the exemplar of realism in English fiction? Defoe was a Realist, or at least a realistic writer, in the best sense of the word. But he is no more a Realist than is Fielding, or Thackeray, or Jane Austen.

229

I think no one who knows what realistic writing is will deny that it is to be found in the works, not only of the three authors just named, but also in those of Charlotte Brontë, George Eliot, and Thomas Hardy; and I think no critic who understands his business will place *A Child of the Jago* in the same class with *Vanity Fair, Barry Lyndon, Catherine, Silas Marner, Jane Eyre, Tess of the D'Urbervilles,* and *Sense and Sensibility.* Let any admirer of Mr. Morrison's who feels inclined to disagree with me here read the gambling scene in *Catherine,* the chapter in *Vanity Fair* wherein Rawden Crawley finds the Marquis of Steyne with his wife; the drawing of lots in the Lantern Yard Chapel in *Silas Marner;* the account of Jane Eyre's childhood, or the school scenes in *Villette;* the military scenes in *Barry Lyndon;* the rape, the murder, or the basket-making in *Tess;* and the tavern scenes in *Janet's Repentance,* and I think he will admit that *A Child of the Jago* has no more right to pose as the greatest piece of realistic fiction since Defoe than

230

Rudyard Kipling's *Seven Seas* have to be
called the noblest poems since Milton.

As to the discovery of a new country in
our very midst. What is this new country?
It is a district of Shoreditch—a small area of
London slums. Has Mr. Morrison discovered
the London slums? What about Douglas
Jerrold, Charles Dickens, Henry Kingsley,
Walter Besant, Rudyard Kipling, and
George Gissing? Have you ever read
Oliver Twist, The Nether World, Ravenshoe,
or *The Record of Baddalia Herodsfoot?*

As to Mr. Morrison's founding a new
school of realistic fiction, what about Stephen
Crane, Kipling, and Gissing? Is not
"Jago Court" exactly the same place as
Kipling's "Gunnison Street" and Henry
Kingsley's "Marquis Court"? Are not the
Ranns and the Learys, and their faction
fights, own brothers to the Moriartys and
the O'Neils in *Ravenshoe?* Is not the
moral of Mr. Morrison's story, and is not
the hero of his story, anticipated in Jerrold's
St. Giles and St. James? Read the burglary,
the murder, the reflections of Josh Perrot

at the trial and after, the flight of Dicky Perrot with the musical box, and the attempts of Josh Perrot to escape from the police, and then read the burglary, the murder, the reflections of Fagin in court, the flight of Oliver from the bookstall, and the efforts of Bill Sikes to get away over the roof in Jacob's Island, and tell me what you think of the French critic's claim that a new school of fiction has been founded by Mr. Morrison. After Victor Hugo's Garroche, George Gissing's Pennyloaf Candy, Rudyard Kipling's Lascar Loo, Stephen Crane's Maggie, Dickens's Bill Sikes, Rogue Riderhood, Artful Dodger, Flash Toby Crockitt, and Fagin, what is there in Dicky Perrot, in Pigeony Poll, in Josh Perrot, in Bill Rann, in Weech, to startle us by its novelty? Don't our critics read anything, I wonder; or do they forget what they read?

The moral of *A Child of the Jago* is a sound moral, but it is not new. It is the moral that children born and bred in the " Jago " will develop into " Jago rats." That such children have no chance to be

232

aught but thieves or harlots. I think you'll find the same moral in *Merrie England.* I think, to go farther back, you'll find it in *St. Giles and St. James*; indeed, I will quote it in Douglas Jerrold's own words—

It has been my endeavour to show in the person of St. Giles (the child of St. Giles's) the victim of an ignorant disregard of the social claims of the poor upon the rich; of the governed millions upon the governing few; to present the picture of the infant pauper reared in brutish ignorance; a human waif of dirt and darkness.

And again—

Consider this little *man*. Are not creatures such as these the noblest, grandest things of earth? Have they not solemn natures—are they not subtly touched for the highest purposes of human life? . . . There is no spot, no coarser stuff in the pauper flesh before you, that indicates a lower nature. There is no felon mark upon it — no natural formation indicating the thief in its baby fingers—no inevitable blasphemy upon its lips. It lies before you a fair unsullied thing, fresh from the Hand of God. Will you, without an effort, let the great fiend stamp his fiery brand upon it? Shall it, even in its sleeping innocence, be made a trading thing by misery and

233

vice? A creature borne from street to street, a piece of ragged living merchandise for mingled beggary and crime? Say what with its awakening soul shall it learn? What lessons whereby to pass through life making an item in the social sum? Why, cunning will be its wisdom; hypocrisy its truth; theft its natural law of self-preservation. To this child, so nurtured, so taught, your whole code of morals, nay, your brief right and wrong, are writ in stranger figures than Egyptian hieroglyphs, and—time passes —and you scourge the creature never taught for the heinous guilt of knowing naught but ill! The good has been a sealed book to him, and the dunce is punished with the jail.

That is the moral of *A Child of the Jago*, and it is the moral of *St. Giles and St. James.*

And now I am going to quote the faction fight in Marquis Court, from *Ravenshoe*, firstly because it resembles the faction fights in the "Jago"; secondly, because it is a piece of sterling realism; thirdly, because it contains an overflowing, genial humour, in which Mr. Morrison's book is lacking. This is a battle in the night—

The court was silent and hushed, when, from the door exactly opposite to Malone's there appeared a tall and rather handsome young man, with a great frieze coat under one arm, and a fire-shovel over his shoulder.

This was Mr. Dennis Moriarty, junior. He advanced to the arch, and then walked down the centre of the court, dragging the coat behind him, lifting his heels defiantly high at every step, and dexterously beating "a chune on the bare head of um wid the fire-shovel. Hurroo!"

He had advanced half-way down the court without a soul appearing, when suddenly the enemy poured out on him in two columns from behind two doorways, and he was borne back, fighting like a hero with his fire-shovel, into one of the doors on his own side of the court.

The two columns of the enemy, headed by Mr. Phelim O'Neil, uniting, poured into the doorway after him, and from the interior of the house arose a hubbub exactly as though people were fighting on the stairs.

At this point there happened one of those mistakes which so often occur in warfare, which are disastrous at the time, and inexplicable afterwards. Can anyone explain why Lord Lucan gave that order at Balaclava? No. Can anyone explain to me why on this occasion Mr. Phelim O'Neil headed the attack on the staircase in person, leaving his rear struggling in confusion in the court, by reason of their hearing the fun going on inside, and not being able to get at it. I think not. Such was the case, however, and in the midst of it, Mr. Malone, howling like a demon, and horribly drunk, followed by thirty or forty worse than himself, dashed out of a doorway close by, and before they had time to form line of battle, fell upon them hammer and tongs.

I need not say that after this surprise in the rear, Mr. Phelim O'Neil's party had very much the worst of it. In about ten minutes, however, the two parties were standing opposite one another once more, inactive from sheer fatigue.

At this moment Miss Ophelia Flanigan appeared from the door of No. 8, and slowly and majestically advanced towards the rostrum in front of her own door, and, ascending the steps, folded her arms and looked about her.

She was an uncommonly powerful red-faced Irishwoman; her arms were bare, and she had them akimbo, and was scratching her elbows.

Every schoolboy knows that the lion has a claw at the end of his tail with which he lashes himself into fury. When the experienced hunter sees him doing that, he, so to speak, "hooks it." When Miss Flanigan's enemies saw her scratching her elbows, they generally did the same. She was scratching her elbows now. There was a dead silence.

One woman in that court, and one only, ever offered battle to the terrible Miss Ophelia; that was young Mrs. Phalim O'Nale. On the present occasion she began slowly walking up and down in front of the expectant hosts. While Miss O'Flanigan looked on

236

in contemptuous pity, scratching her elbows, Mrs. O'Neil opened fire.

"Pussey, Pussey!" she began, "Kitty, Kitty, Kitty! Miaow, Miaow!" (Mr. Malone had accumulated property in the cats' meat business.) "Morraow, ye little tabby divvle, don't come anighst her, my Kitleen Avourneen, or ye'll be converted into sassidge mate, an' sould to kape a drunken one-eyed old rapparee, from the County Cork, as had two months for bowling his barrer sharp round the corner of Park Lane over a ould gineral officer, in a white hat and a green silk umbrella; and as married a red-haired woman from the County Waterford, as calls herself by her maiden name, and never feels up to fightin' but when the licker's in her, which it most in general is, pussey; an' let me see the one of Malone's lot, or Moriarty's lot ather, for that matter, as will deny it. Miaow!"

That is as true and forcible a picture as any in the "Jago," and more humorous. By the way, there is a slum boy in Ravenshoe of similar character to Dicky Perrot.

Mr. George Gissing's pictures of London life and the London poor are more comprehensive than Mr. Morrison's. I think they give a completer, though even more gloomy, view of lower London than that in *A Child*

237

of the Jago. Henry Kingsley is Mr.
Morrison's equal in knowledge and in style,
and his superior in humour; Dickens is his
master at all points. But the story which
comes nearest to *A Child of the Jago* in
subject and treatment is Mr. Kipling's *Record
of Baddalia Herodsfoot.* The resemblance
between these two tales is remarkable, and
it must be confessed that in point of style,
of force, of originality, and of atmosphere,
the work of "the most consummate master
of realistic fiction since Defoe" is excelled
by that of the young man from the country.
Kipling's story is much shorter, but it is so
concentrated and so vivid that it seems to
contain more than Mr. Morrison's. It
contains also many of those terse, pregnant
sentences which Mr. Kipling strikes out as
a born sculptor strikes out a face on a stick
with a few cuts of a knife, to the wonder and
envy of journeymen carvers without genius.
Thus, of the pregnant Jenny and her (brevet)
husband, he says, " The shapelessness of her
figure revolted him, and he said as much,
in the language of his breed." And Jenny,

238

taking to liquor, tells a neighbour, "When your man drinks, you'd better drink too! It don't 'urt so much when 'e 'its you then." And again, the same Jenny says to her husband, "You call yourself a man—you call yourself the bleedin' shadow of a man? I've seen better men than you made outer chewed paper." And the policeman says to Jenny, "Well, if you *are* a married woman, cover up your breasts."

Then when Baddalia is knocked down, and Tom kicks her, he "kicks with deadly intelligence born of whisky"; and Jenny threatens Baddalia in this wise: "An' you, Baddalia, I'll tear your face off its bones"; and Lascar Loo's mother knew that "hell has no fury like a woman fighting above the life that is quick in her." Note also the significance of Jenny's exclamation when Tom is arrested after kicking Baddalia to death: "Took for a common drunk. Gawd send they don't look at 'is boots"; and the following sentence from the ramblings of the dying woman: "If Tom 'ad come back, which 'e never did, I'd ha' been like the

239

rest—sixpence for beef-tea for the baby, an'
a shillin' for layin' out the baby."

Such phrasing as this is born, not made,
in a man. Those words are poignant; they
stick deep, and stay long. One could not
in many years forget the closing words of
Kipling's powerful story, where the "dying
prostitute who cannot die" is wailing to her
thief of a mother, who has stolen her
custard, "Oh, mother, mother, won't you
even let me lick the spoon?" I have looked
in vain for any such verbal jewellery as this
in *A Child of the Jago.*

On second thoughts, I shall not waste
time in proving that Mr. Morrison's genius
is not higher and purer than that of Defoe.
Firstly, because Defoe needs no champion;
and secondly, because I don't think Mr.
Morrison has any genius at all. Talent he
has, industry he has, and a sound knowledge
of his subject and his craft; but of genius
the *Child of the Jago* affords no gleam. It
is a clever book, a true book, a useful book,
but it is in nowise great. The characters
are natural, and well drawn, but they are

not new nor masterly creations ; the dialogue is terse and clean-cut, but it is not strikingly original, like that of Dickens — there is a strange absence of Cockney wit. The action is quick, the descriptions are graphic, the style is clear, virile, and workman-like; but I can think of nothing in the book which could not have been as well done by any one of a dozen living English authors.

But there is no man in the world who could write anything like *Barry Lyndon, Jane Eyre, Robinson Crusoe, Great Expectations, Silas Marner, Tom Jones, Les Miserables,* or *Vanity Fair.* We remember such characters as Becky Sharp, Silas Marner, Squire Western, Jean Valjean, Mrs. Gargery, and Barry Lyndon as great and distinctive human figures; we remember the speeches and sallies of Sam Weller, of Tony Weller, of Mrs. Poyser, of Rawdon Crawley, of Richard Swiveller, as we remember the humour of Shakespeare's clowns and of the gravediggers in *Hamlet*; and we search in vain for any such original types or original dialogue in the work of Mr. Morrison. No. *A Child of the Jago* is a good book, and well worth reading; but it has not one element of greatness nor one stroke of genius in all its pages. The "Jago" people never surprise one, never delight one, never shock one, never make one laugh. There are smiles in the book, and sighs; but no laughter, no tears. It contains nothing of such stabbing pathos as Joe's "He was werry good to me, he wos," nothing so startling and dramatic as the footprint on Crusoe's sand, nothing to surprise the heart into laughter like the cry of Tony Weller, "Samivel, Samivel, why weren't there a halibi?" or the blurted acknow- ledgment of the professional perjurer, when asked what he was prepared to swear, "In a general way, hanythink," or the solemn statement of Mr. Wegg that "nothing is more mellerin' to the horgans than a weal an' 'ammer." No, *A Child of the Jago* will not set the Thames on fire. By the way, I think the last words of Dicky Perrot ring false: "Tell Mr. Beveridge there's another way out —better." There speaks the artful author, striving for an effect, not the "Jago rat" dying from a stab in the lung.

Mr. Morrison has been applauded for his clever interpretation of Josh Perrot's mind during the trial, and while under sentence of death, and it has, I think, been generally conceded that this part of Mr. Morrison's book affords an example of realism at its best.

The exposition of Josh Perrot's mind and process of thought in his time of peril and suspense is very artistic, and so plausible that at first it convinces one of its truth; but *is* it true? I don't think it is true, I don't think it is realistic; and I will give my reasons for the doubt.

The reflections and mental state of Perrot are, of course, an expansion and development of the much-admired picture of Fagin under like conditions.

It was an inspiration of genius which made Dickens show Fagin interested, or at least observant of the trivialities around him, in his hour of danger and deadly fear. You remember how he watched the artist who was sketching him, and wondered whether the likeness would be a good one; and how he noticed the Judge's dress, and wondered what it cost and how he put it on; and how he thought of the fat man who had been out to dinner, and wondered what he had had and where he had been to get it. Then you will remember, also, that Dickens says—

Not that, all this time, his mind was, for an instant, free from one oppressive, overwhelming sense of the grave that opened at his feet; it was ever present to him, but in a vague and general way, and he could not fix his thoughts upon it. Thus, even while he trembled, and turned burning hot at the idea of speedy death, he fell to counting the iron spikes before him, and wondering how the head of one had been broken off, and whether they would mend it or leave it as it was. Then he thought of all the horrors of the gallows and the scaffold, and stopped to watch a man sprinkling the floor to cool it, and then went on to think again.

Next let us take a glance at Josh Perrot in the dock—

The lion and unicorn had been fresh gilt since he was there before, but the white-headed old jailer in the dock was much the same. And the big sword—

what did they have a big sword for, stuck up there, over the red cushions, and what was the use of a sword six foot long? But perhaps it wasn't six foot after all; it looked longer than it was, and no doubt it was only for show, and probably a dummy with no blade. There was a well-dressed black man sitting down below among the lawyers. What did he want? Why did they let him in? A nice thing—to be made a show of, for niggers! And Josh Perrot loosened his neckcloth with an indignant tug of the forefinger, and went off into another train of thought. He had a throbbing, wavering headache, the outcome of thinking so hard about so many things. They were small things, and had nothing to do with his own business; but there were so many of them, *and they all had to be got through at such a pace, and one thing led to another.*

The italics are mine, put there to mark passages which seem to me of special merit.

Ever since they had taken him he had been oppressed by this plague of galloping thought, with few intervals of rest, when he could consider immediate concerns. But of these he made little trouble. The thing was done. Very well, then, he would take his gruel like a man. He had done many a worse thing, he said, that had been thought less of.

The evidence was a nuisance. What was the good —————? Over and over and over again. At the inquest, at the police-court, and now here. Repeated, laboriously taken down, and repeated again. And now it was worse than ever, for the judge insisted on making a note of everything, and wrote it down slowly, a word at a time. The witnesses were like barrel-organs, producing the same old tune mechanically, without changing a note. There was the policeman who was in Meakin Street at twelve-thirty on the morning of the fourth of the month, when he heard cries of Murder, and proceeded to the coffee shop. There was the other policeman who also "proceeded" there, and recognised the prisoner, whom he knew, at the first-floor window. And there was the sergeant who had found him in the cellar, and the doctor who had made an examination, and the knife, and the boots, and all of it. It was Murder, Murder, Murder still. Why? Wasn't it plain enough? He felt some interest in what was coming— in the sentence, and the black cap, and so on—never having seen a murder trial before. But all this repetition oppressed him vaguely amid the innumerable things he had to think of, one thing leading to another.

All this is excellent writing, and sounds startlingly real. Let us take a few lines describing Josh on the morning of his execution—

Yes, yes, of course, they always tolled a bell. But it was rather confusing, with things to think about.

Ah, they had come at last. Come, there was nothing more to think about now; nothing but to take it game. Hold tight, Jago, hold tight.

. . . "No thank you, sir—nothing to say, special. On'y much obliged to ye, thank ye kindly, for the grub an'—an' bein' kind an' wot not. Thanks all of ye, come to that. Specially you, sir." It was the tall black figure again. . . .

What, this was the chap, was it? Seedy-looking. Sort of undertaker's man to look at. All right—straps. Not cords to tie, then. Waist; wrists; elbows; more straps dangling below—do them presently. This was how they did it then. . . . This way?

"I am the resurrection and the life, saith the Lord: he that believeth in Me, though he were dead, yet shall he live: and whosoever liveth and believeth in Me shall never die."

A very big gate this, all iron, painted white. Round to the right. Not very far, they told him. It was dark in the passage, but the door led into the yard, where it was light and open, and sparrows were twittering. Another door: in a shed.

This was the place. All white, everywhere—frame too; not black after all. Up the steps. . . . Hold tight: not much longer. Stand there? Very well.

"Man that is born of a woman hath but a short time to live, and is full of misery. He cometh up, and is cut down, like a flower: he fleeth, as it were a shadow, and never continueth in one stay.

"In the midst of life" . . .

All very clever, and all true—but not all the truth. Josh Perrot would see all those things, and think all those things—but would he think nothing else? He was a brave, determined, and ignorant man, but he had imagination, as is evidenced in his words to Weech just before the murder, and in his reflections during flight just after the murder.

I mean to say that Perrot would think all Mr. Morrison makes him think, but that he would also think, and think chiefly, of his peril and his death.

Dickens makes Fagin think of the gallows and the grave; but only as an undercurrent to his trivial thoughts, and only in spasms; but Perrot scarcely thinks of death at all, or else Mr. Morrison meant to imply that Perrot crushes the more awful thought wilfully, and by dint of wilful persistence in thoughts about minor matters.

Now, I believe I am right in saying that Fagin and Perrot both would think all the

248

time of their trial, persistently, earnestly, and anxiously, of their own immediate danger, but that all the while they were thinking of the great matter, they would be abnormally conscious of the small matters.

Have you ever been in great peril? I remember a case of my own. I once climbed a high, perpendicular chalk cliff, and when within a dozen feet of the top found I could go no farther. I am horribly afraid of falling: it is the terror of my life. My flesh creeps at the thought. And there I hung by my fingers and toes three hundred feet above the rocks, with the rotten chalk crumbling under my weight. It was a lovely summer's day; and I was twenty years of age. Behind me was the blue sea, and above me the silky, sunny sky. And Death had his chilly hand upon my shoulder. My fingers were bleeding. I could feel my feet breaking away the risky hold on the chalk. I could hear my heart beat. I could hear my friend singing as he gathered shellfish from the rocks below me — the rocks on which I might soon be smashed and killed.

I looked down; the friend looked like a doll. The rocks were horribly sharp and cruel. I turned sick and cold, and the sweat ran over me. I shook so that I could scarcely hold on, and I felt a wild impulse to shut my eyes and jump into death. All this within a couple of seconds.

And what did I think? I thought that I should be mad to leave go. I thought that I *must* control my nerve and be cool. I thought that I must go down very, very cautiously. I said to myself, "Steady, steady! don't be a coward. What are you afraid of? It is only death." These are the things I *thought*.

But what did I see, and notice, and become conscious of? I remembered all my friends and many of the scenes I had passed through—holidays, nights of sickness, journeys, adventures! And I noticed everything within range of my senses. The smell of the seaweed, the shrill calling of the gulls, the warmth of the sun on my back, the high lights on the tiny tufts of grass in the crevice of the cliff, the yellow lights and the c blue shadows of the small lumps of chalk with which the cliff-face was studded, the queer resemblance of the sound made by my own heart-throbs to that produced by a small steam pump in a shop where I had once been working. All these things I noticed. But I never stopped thinking of my danger and of how I was to get down, and I never thought of the gulls and the grass and the lights and shades of the chalk crumbs *in words*.

And there is the question: Would Josh Perrot and Fagin think in words of the trivial things about them? I don't think they would. They would be conscious of those things; but all the while they would be *thinking* of death, of their chances of eluding, or of their powers of enduring death.

However, I have exceeded my limits, and must quit the subject. Yet, before I lay down the pen I'd like to say a word about Defoe.

Defoe is always held up as the realist of realists, and we are always being told about Defoe's wealth of detail. Now, the good

Daniel did use detail, but he used it with consummate art; with a fatal precision of selection so that every detail helped the picture, — and meant something, — just as every line of Albert Durer's in a drawing meant something. Defoe not only understood the realistic effect of detail, he understood the artistic use and the artistic selection of detail. Why, even the list of the things he took from the wreck reads like a wild sea song, so picturesquely are the items grouped, so cleverly are they selected, with such magic are they displayed in an atmosphere of romance, and upon a background of sea and sky and wreckage, and the strange wild island.

But compare Defoe's detail with that of the modern spurious realist. Take an instance. When Crusoe rescues the Spaniard, no less than twenty-one savages are shot. Now remember what modern realism is; remember how some modern authors use detail; remember how much has been said about Defoe's realism and love of detail, and then ponder these facts.

252

Those twenty-one savages are killed without our seeing a drop of blood, or hearing one shriek or groan. We don't know whether they are hit in the body or the head. We can say nothing of their dying agonies, or the contortions of the features, or the writhing of their limbs. We don't know whether they fall upon their faces or their backs. And we are surprised to remember that they are never buried.

But I really dare not write any more, and so good-bye.

www.ingramcontent.com/pod-product-compliance
Ingram Content Group UK Ltd.
Pitfield, Milton Keynes, MK11 3LW, UK
UKHW021326151224
3677UKWH00046B/573